How to do good

ESSAYS ON BUILDING A BETTER WORLD

LONDON WALL PUBLISHING

Edited by Andrew White & Joanne Bladd
Design by Matt Walker

Leonard Stall
CEO & Editor-in-chief
leonard@touchline.ae

Waleed ElTayeb Gubara
COO & Partner

Salem AlShaikh
Publishing Director, Philanthropy Age

Anas Albounni
Production Manager

With special thanks to:
Adrienne Cernigoi, Liam Yeoh & Linda Musco

Philanthropy Age
Touchline FZ LLC
TwoFour54 Media Zone
Abu Dhabi, UAE

First published in the UK in 2016 by
London Wall Publishing Ltd (LWP)

First published in eBook edition in the UK in 2016 by
London Wall Publishing Ltd (LWP)

London Wall Publishing Ltd (LWP)
24 Chiswell Street, London EC1Y 4YX

Printed in the UK by Bensson Group

A CIP catalogue record for this book is
available from the British Library.

ISBN 978-0-9932917-8-4

'How to do good' is brought to you by the team at Philanthropy Age, a quarterly print and digital edition magazine that sets out to inspire and inform intelligent giving, and to celebrate the great initiatives, fieldwork, foundations and individuals making a difference in our world.

You can find out more at philanthropyage.com

Writers and contributors

Essays on building a better world

How to do good

An introduction

––––––––

'How to do good' is a celebration of thoughtfulness and shared humanity. Each of our contributors is making a positive difference in today's challenged world: from European and Middle Eastern royalty, to a former US president who commands international respect, and one half of the world's wealthiest couple and the highest-profile advocates for effective philanthropy. Our writers are Hollywood icons, and also the heads of some of the world's largest foundations and humanitarian bodies. They are successful businesspeople and dynamic social entrepreneurs. They are everyday people doing truly extraordinary things.

Taken together, these exclusive essays and interviews show us all what can be achieved given vision and determination, and whatever our individual circumstances. Thank you to everyone involved.

This book is dedicated to the amazing people we meet every day through our work at Philanthropy Age, who show time and time again that everyone can make a difference. Yet, in this instance I found inspiration in a country leader from the Gulf, a ruler who rarely makes the international headlines, His Highness Sheikh Sabah Al-Ahmad Al-Jaber Al-Sabah, the Amir of Kuwait.

The Amir's ongoing dedication to helping refugees sits as part of a lifetime's humanitarian work. Although Ban ki-moon, as UN secretary general, honoured the Amir as a Humanitarian Leader in 2014, much of his remarkable contribution is deliberately low-key, like the work of so many of our contributors.

The Amir has galvanised huge financial assistance from around the globe to support relief efforts for refugees, particularly those from Syria and Iraq. His work is a testament to genuine humanity, and a lesson in compassion and understanding for leaders worldwide at a time when the weight of humanitarian crises is more acute and distressing than ever.

Our own story, as the publishers of Philanthropy Age, is proof positive that determination and willpower counts when it comes to 'doing good'. Four years ago we decided to launch a magazine to inspire and inform intelligent giving. We wanted our new title to try and coax donors away from random acts of charity, and towards more planned strategic giving, which typically has a far greater impact.

Today, we publish print editions worldwide in English and Arabic, along with interactive multi-language digital editions for different regions, and a growing website. We have conducted respected independent research into the giving behaviour of Arabs in the Gulf, partnered with organisations such as UN Women to amplify messages of global importance, and become a grantee of the Bill & Melinda Gates Foundation, which has inspired us to do even more.

Our team does this work as not-for-profit alongside our normal day-to-day business. It is our own contribution to 'doing good' and building a better world. It is something we will be proud to tell our grandchildren, and we hope that this book will be the first of many such inspirational projects.

Leonard Stall

Editor-in-chief

Closing the gap

Phumzile Mlambo-Ngcuka

Around the world, in every community, women are paid less than men even when they perform equally valuable jobs, writes UN Women executive director Phumzile Mlambo-Ngcuka. If the world hopes to eradicate extreme poverty, it must change the way it values work – and equal pay must lead the agenda

———————

Phumzile Mlambo-Ngcuka
Executive director, UN Women

————

THE AUTHOR

Phumzile Mlambo-Ngcuka is the executive director of UN Women, which was founded in 2010 to be the UN's global champion for women and girls. A former deputy president of South Africa, she has devoted her career to issues of human rights, equality and social justice, and was actively involved in the struggle to end apartheid in her home country

——

W omen, on average across the world, are paid 24 per cent less than men. The women in those jobs are not 24 per cent less able, less experienced or less qualified. They are just 100 per cent less male. Pay inequality based on gender persists everywhere, across countries, regions and occupations, and it matters. It matters because it is an evident injustice and because it condemns millions of women and their families to lives of entrenched poverty. It is a global, systemic problem that needs concerted attention and action to change the way that we value and support women's work.

Race and ethnicity compounds the disparity. Though data is scarce in developing countries, in the US, for example, African American women earn only $0.60, Native American women $0.59 and Latinas $0.55 for every $1 that white men earn.

The gender pay gap has obvious immediate repercussions – but also relates directly to longer-term impacts such as women's credit-worthiness, savings, social security benefits and retirement income. Globally, some 200 million women in old age are living without any regular income from an old age or survivor's pension, despite having been in the workforce in earlier life.

Where every dollar counts, pay inequality can be enough to plunge families below the breadline. Insufficient income reinforces the poverty cycle, limits opportunity and entrenches disadvantage. A sufficient income well spent on education, nutrition and health potentially moves a generation out of poverty.

All over the world, women are paid less than men for the same job and their work is seen as being less valuable. Janitors (mostly a male job) are paid more than maids (mostly a female job) yet their job descriptions are virtually identical. In the US, golf caddies (who are mostly men) earn an average of $17 an hour;

Phumzile Mlambo-Ngcuka

"Globally, women do two and a half times more unpaid work and domestic work as men"

———

while caregivers (mostly women) are paid just $9 an hour. Why should carrying golf clubs be worth so much more than carrying children? The discrepancies illustrate a problem of perception, reflecting unquestioned assumptions of relative value that have complex and damaging ramifications.

Women are typically employed in low-paid sectors, in caring for children and the elderly, in domestic work, cleaning and catering. In professional positions, more women than men are employed in the lower-paid roles, such as primary school teachers and nurses, rather than as more highly valued university lecturers and engineers. Even as lawyers, judges, surgeons or aircraft pilots, women are paid less than their male counterparts for the same job.

This consistent undervaluation is a key driver of the gender pay gap. It has two aspects: women are underpaid in the jobs that they do, and the jobs that they do are valued less because they are seen as 'women's work'. Both constrain women's ability to earn.

As women are paid less, they must work longer hours to net the same income. Yet demands at home often mean they must work fewer hours than their male counterparts, or find ways to subcontract their care duties to others. The pay gap therefore underpins a vast, almost invisible care workforce and a little recognised care economy. Globally, women do two and a half times more unpaid care and domestic work as men. The economic value of this work is estimated to be anywhere between 15 per cent of GDP in South Africa, to a staggering 39 per cent of GDP in India.

The reality of the 'male breadwinner' is long gone, but it has not been replaced by a viable alternative. Contemporary economies need both men and women to work, but employment is often designed as if there were no responsibilities at home.

In order to be able to take a job, women may opt to pay others to provide care for their families. This can result in a complicated cascade of sub-contracted care, in which each working mother spends a proportion of her earnings on paying for another woman to tend her household, who in turn may well have to do the same in order to free up time to earn. But who looks after the children of working women who cannot afford or have no access to this essential support? In surveys of 31 developing countries, just 4 per cent of employed women had access to a nursery, while 39 per cent said that they themselves look after their children.

Failure to support the care economy reinforces the gender pay gap in two ways: by undervaluing women's jobs and entrenching women in low-paid work; and by limiting women's paid work opportunities, through a lack of affordable care services.

The current reality is that women must either take on poor quality, part-time or informal work that they can combine with childcare duties, or entrust that care to family members. This can have a high cost of its own. In developing countries with poor infrastructure and no formal care services, girls may be forced to drop out of secondary school to fetch water or fuel, and take care of younger siblings or elderly family members, at the expense of their education and a better future. It is time to call a halt to this broken system. It is clear that the loop of low pay and reliance on unsupported family care is undesirable and unsustainable.

One promising solution is government investment in care services. A study by the International Trade Union Confederation and the Women's Budget Group in the UK found that investing in a universal, free childcare system, in which workers are paid a decent wage, would create 1.65 million jobs and reduce the gender pay gap by 3.4 per cent. Children would get the best start in life, women could stay in the labour market and build their careers, and best of all, most of the investment would be recouped through increased tax revenues and lower welfare spending. Some Latin American countries, including Ecuador, Mexico and Chile, have started to make real progress on childcare services in recent years. These services are costly, especially in the short term, but they are an economic and social investment that yields rich returns.

Elsewhere governments are tackling the gender pay gap head on. In the UK, the government announced an ambition to end the gender pay gap within a generation, making companies with more than 250 workers disclose the pay gap in their workplaces. Such

'Why should carrying golf clubs be worth more than carrying children? The discrepancies illustrate a problem of perception'

transparency can make a difference. In 11 US states, pay secrecy
is unlawful. A study found that in those states, the gender wage
gap is smaller and women tend to earn more than in other states.

Increased minimum wages at national level is another avenue,
with disproportionate benefits for low paid women. Corporate
policies such as parental leave, flexible working hours and working
from home are growing, although the changes in culture that make
uptake feasible still lag. There are no simple answers, and economic
empowerment for women is just one aspect of full gender equality.
But when it comes to tackling the gender pay gap, we urgently need
to be finding and implementing effective solutions. ○

"Where every dollar counts, pay inequality can be enough to plunge families below the breadline"

Phumzile Mlambo-Ngcuka

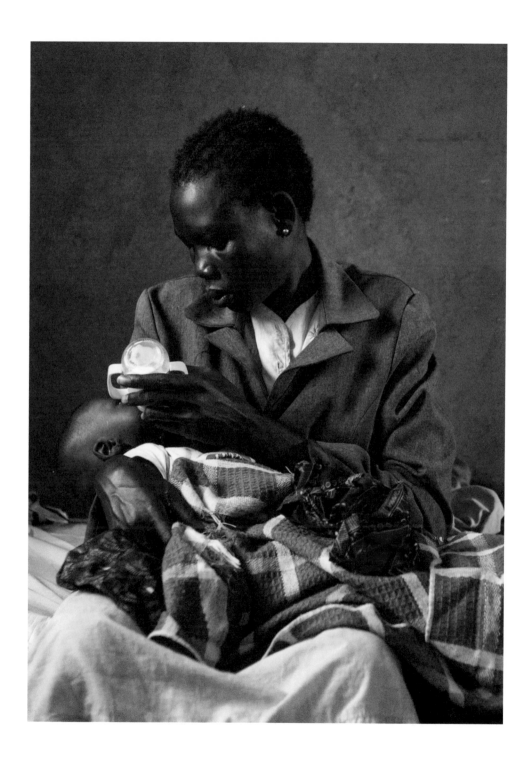

Second take

Matt Damon

Sometimes, passion for a cause is just not enough. When you want to be successful at making a difference for millions of people around the world, don't be afraid to rip up the script, learn to be a student again, and enlist a little expert help to do it better the second time around, says actor and humanitarian Matt Damon

Matt Damon
Actor, cofounder Water.org

THE AUTHOR

Matt Damon is an actor, writer
and humanitarian. In 2009 he
cofounded Water.org, an initiative
dedicated to improving access
to clean water and sanitation for
impoverished communities in
Africa and South Asia. He has also
been active on behalf of other
charitable organisations including
the ONE Campaign and ONEXONE

W here I grew up you just had to walk over to the tap and turn it on; we were never thirsty, and I didn't know anyone who was. So I found it very hard to relate when I learned that in some parts of the world, kids were dying of diseases to which the cure was essentially clean water. People talk about the global water crisis and what's coming down the road. Yet for 660 million people, that crisis is already here.

Back in 2006 I knew I wanted to engage with issues of extreme poverty, and I knew there were a range of pressing problems that I needed to understand more about. On a fact-finding mission to Africa, I spent a day learning about the impact water has on poverty, and I was shocked and amazed that more people back home in America weren't talking about it. At that time the US had a big engagement on AIDS, and yet a lack of access to clean water was killing far more children worldwide.

I started out taking a closer look at some of the worst affected areas, and also pushing funding to some people who were doing some really good work in this field. There was so much low-hanging fruit, so many people who were affected by this, that my thinking was that if I could raise the money to sink a few bore wells, then I could reach a certain amount of people.

H2O Africa launched in Spring 2006. Even at the time I knew it wasn't the most sophisticated way of attacking the problem, but I wanted to do something. We didn't make the perfect the enemy of the good, and so we just jumped in and found people who were doing work we believed in, and raised money so they could continue doing that work.

It didn't take me long to realise a couple of things. The first was that we were attacking the problem in the wrong way, and the second

'I realised pretty
quickly that if we
joined forces we
could do so much
more together than
separately. In 2009
I approached Gary
[White] with my hat
in my hand'

was that we could do much better on an organisational level, too. Before long I had reached a point where I looked at the scale of the problem and I looked at my efforts, and I knew I had two choices: give up, or start over.

For a philanthropist, or for anyone interested in making a positive difference to the world, that's really the important moment, because that's when you have to go for it. You tell yourself that you have something to offer, and that if you re-examine what you're doing and try and go about it in a different way, then maybe you can really move the needle. Half the water projects in the world fail, and I was very aware of that. What I needed was to learn from the successful projects, to find someone who could show me where I was going wrong, and guide me on this difficult but important journey.

Gary White was founder of WaterPartners, a nonprofit group with a great record. They were very smart about how they operated and I realised pretty quickly that if we joined forces we could do so much more together, than separately. In 2009 I approached Gary with my hat in my hand. I said I wanted to help and that I felt I could do more, and I think he saw an opportunity whereby we could reach a lot more people if we did it together. Since that moment Water.org, of which Gary and I are cofounders, has reached more than 3.3 million people, through 56 programmes in 12 countries. We have worked with more than 60 partner organisations and leveraged more than $12m in philanthropic subsidies to attract $128m in commercial and social capital to provide water supply and sanitation loans. We're making a difference to millions of people who otherwise couldn't afford to access clean water.

I'm also learning new things every day. Gary has three engineering degrees and more than two decades of experience in the field. I'll never be that guy, but in terms of the issue I can go to school on it and that's what I have done. I'm learning constantly and I think that's really important for anybody considering becoming involved in philanthropy: give yourself permission to be a student. Even Gary, who is an absolute expert in this field, is always asking questions on our trips because conditions are changing constantly.

Today, more kids are dying from a lack of access to clean water than from AIDS, measles and malaria combined. It's the most serious problem out there, and we need to approach it just as seriously. I chose water because of its enormity and its complexity: it looked like something that I could engage with over my entire life, and that has certainly turned out to be the case. If I'm on a movie I'm working 15 hours a day, but if I'm not I'm with my family or I'm with Water.org.

People who go into philanthropy are often very successful in other areas of life, and I think it can be embarrassing to be the student again. Yet I would encourage anyone thinking about this, that that's really the fun of it. Once you give yourself permission to not know everything, then that's when life gets exciting again. ○

"It can be embarrassing to be the student again. Yet I would encourage anyone thinking about it, that that's the fun of it"

Matt Damon

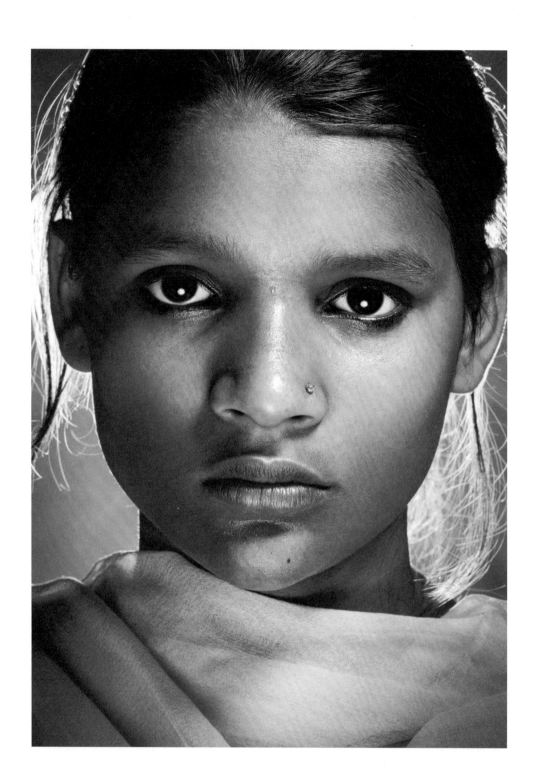

Educating India

Azim Premji

Azim Premji is India's most generous man having spent the last two decades committing a vast proportion of his wealth to social causes through his eponymous foundation. He describes his personal giving journey, his mission to transform public education, and hails the emergence of a new generation of Indian philanthropists

———

Azim Premji
Chairman, Wipro

––––––––

THE CONTRIBUTOR

Azim Premji is the chairman of IT
giant Wipro, one of India's largest
publicly traded companies.
He launched the Azim Premji
Foundation in 2001, and has since
transferred more than $8bn of his
personal wealth to the foundation
to support social causes. This
essay was composed from an
interview with Mr Premji

––––

I had a very simple idea when I started: what could I do to contribute to a better India, a just, equitable and humane India as envisaged in the constitution?

I became responsible for Wipro in the late 1960s, and for three decades dedicated myself almost completely to building the business. In that time I travelled extensively within the country, and was granted a firsthand view of India's great extremes. For some, rapid development fuelled unimaginable prosperity, while other sections of society remained steeped in poverty and want. I saw that many of the latter lacked even the basic amenities that every human being should have. It felt unfair and wrong. A society must take care of everyone: those who are well-off have a responsibility to do their part to ensure that everyone's basic human needs are met, and that opportunities are created for all, to allow them to develop and grow.

The success of Wipro had made me wealthy; however, I had always considered myself a trustee of that wealth, rather than its owner. Now, as I spoke to family and friends and people within the social sector, I developed clarity in how I wanted to proceed to give a substantial part of my wealth away.

Education stood out clearly as the key building block of a good society. It has a vital role as a transformative force in empowering individuals and communities alike – socially, economically and politically. It is also very clear that children from the most disadvantaged families go into the public school system. We were convinced that to work towards an equitable society, we had to work with the public system.

The thrust of our efforts is to build capacity within the space of public education. We work very closely with all

"I had always considered myself a trustee of my wealth, rather than its owner"

———

levels of the public education system: at the operational level in districts, blocks and clusters, at the level of institutions that support the operations, and at the policy level. We also work on all dimensions of the system, for example from capacity building with teachers and headteachers, to curriculum development, resource material development, assessment reform and more.

To help create real change, we have to work like this – at all levels and on all threads. We have to be there in the difficult areas, and work at the ground level. Such work can't be done from a distance. Today we work in eight states, which have about 350,000 schools, although of course we should remember that India has 1.5 million schools. To achieve this, we have invested in people and built a strong and passionate team at the foundation. If you ask me, that is the single most important factor in the success of any endeavour: building any good operating organisation is not an easy task, and ultimately it boils down to getting good people. By good, I mean people with capability, commitment and tenacity.

The work that needs to be done is not easy, and it needs to be done under very difficult conditions. Working for systemic change is very tough, and it will always be tough.

The rewards, however, make it all worthwhile. It is clear that we are making a genuine contribution to the public education system in India. In order to truly understand this, you have to go to the districts we work in, which are among the most disadvantaged in the country. The changes you see in the teachers, students and government functionaries at the block and cluster level are striking. There is so much energy and enthusiasm, and I witness this firsthand every time I travel to field locations. That's the only way to see the real impact of our work: to meet the teachers, administrators and partners, visit the schools, speak to the students. These moments inspire me and remind me that we must do more.

We hope one day to see an outstanding public education system in the country. When I say 'we', I don't just mean our foundation, but all our partners and the government working together. Philanthropy can never substitute the government's work, as ultimately overall social development requires strong public services, which must be provided by the government. But philanthropy can play a crucial role in helping the public system, in filling gaps the public system is not able to address and in taking on some high-risk projects, which, due to its nature, government cannot fund.

It has to be a team effort as systemic improvements to social issues are complex and take a long time to institute. We don't expect to achieve what we set out for in five or 10 years. We know it is going to take decades, and this is a reality learned and accepted by many Indian business leaders before me. If you study the philanthropic activities of some of the old business families, you will find that they have been working at this for many decades – and in some cases for more than a century – to make a difference in the communities in which they operate.

I am encouraged, nonetheless, by the fact that more and more people are stepping forward to help tackle India's many social challenges. In recent decades we have seen significant new wealth creation in the country, and I see a great seriousness in India's newly wealthy about how to understand and go about addressing social issues.

I feel it is of immense benefit to start an intelligent discourse on personal giving, and so I am trying to engage with this fast-emerging generation of Indian philanthropists in a discreet and thoughtful fashion.

Generally, I refrain from passing on advice and 'telling' people what to do. However, if asked, I will say one thing: social change takes time, and for someone who wishes to make a difference, it is very important to start early. After all, in a country as vast and complex as India, there will always be more to be done. ○

'Education stood
out clearly as the
key building block
of a good society.
It has a vital role
as a transformative
force in empowering
individuals and
communities alike'

Peaceful dividends

Former US President **Jimmy Carter** speaks out on the fight against neglected tropical diseases, the size of the task remaining and why peace and a commitment to human rights is essential for success

———

Jimmy Carter, the 39th US president, is the founder of the Carter Center and the recipient of the 2002 Nobel Peace Prize. Since its inception in 1982 the Carter Center has helped to improve the lives of people in more than 80 countries by resolving conflicts; advancing democracy, human rights and economic opportunity; preventing diseases; improving mental health care; and teaching farmers to increase crop production. Here the former president highlights efforts to combat neglected tropical diseases (NTDs) that affect hundreds of millions of people worldwide – and the battle to eradicate the first human disease since smallpox in 1980.

What progress has been made on NTDs to date?

We at the Carter Center have adopted five of these diseases: Guinea worm, river blindness, trachoma, schistosomiasis and lymphatic filariasis. These diseases have been eliminated in the rich world, and even in much of the middle-income world; a country like Egypt has none of these diseases, for instance. And they are unheard of in Europe, the US and many Arab states. Yet they afflict hundreds of millions of people, causing illness, blindness and worse.

The disease we try most avidly to eradicate is Guinea worm, which is contracted through drinking water from stagnant sources contaminated with the larvae.

People consume the water and imbibe the eggs, and a year later, it grows into a metre-long worm. The worm takes about 30 days to emerge from the human body, causing terrible pain and disfiguration. In 1986, the disease afflicted an estimated 3.5 million people in 21 countries. In 2015, we only saw 22 cases.

We've halted the transmission of river blindness in four countries in central and south America. We've also eliminated or interrupted transmission in 15 out of 17 regions in Uganda, and in one major region in Sudan. We've proved that this can be done, not only in Latin America, but also in Africa.

Trachoma is the world's leading cause of preventable blindness, found in more than 50 countries. It is treated with an antibiotic called Zithromax, which is donated by [pharmaceutical company] Pfizer. In 2015, 16.7 million doses were given through the Carter Center. Of the surgeries carried out globally, to correct eyelid deformities caused by trachoma scarring, the Carter Center supported approximately 45 per cent. We are making good progress.

What is the scale of the remaining challenge?

Much of the challenge is just to be persistent in teaching people in Africa what to do to address their own afflictions, their own diseases. And we have found the people in Africa are so eager to help themselves – they are so hardworking, and ambitious, and want to have better lives. They respond with overwhelming gratitude and dedication.

There is also the difficulty of raising funds. People affected by these diseases are isolated and have little contact with the outside world. Equally, many of those in the developed world don't realise that there is a possibility of preventing or curing these diseases. Finding donors is difficult because they don't understand just how much can be done with minimal financial investment. But the success is there, waiting to be achieved.

What is the economic burden of untreated NTDs?

The cost is high. A World Health Organisation study carried out in a small area of Nigeria showed the cost to the population was close to $20m a year, even in a very poverty-stricken area. The children were unable to attend school, and the farmers – due to sickness – were unable to plant, cultivate or harvest their crops during the harvest season. These diseases can condemn entire communities to poverty.

How do you answer critics who say the elimination of some of these diseases is an unrealistic goal?

These diseases can be eliminated with the right will and funding. We are approaching the point where Guinea worm could be only the second disease ever eradicated from the face of the Earth. It is incredibly hands-on work, yes, and the investment needed is huge. But the results are enormous, and much greater than the effort that is made. We are winning the war.

These diseases are often common in unstable states. To what degree is tackling endemic illnesses a building block to securing lasting peace?

The two are interconnected. Eradicating NTDs depends on whether we can keep the peace. The commitment of the world to the peaceful resolution of differences, and the elevation of human rights to the highest possible level, are key to our progress in the future. Sudan was once one of the worst places on earth for Guinea worm: with the north and south at war, we couldn't access the people affected. In 1995, I went to Sudan with my wife to meet with President Omar al-Bashir in Khartoum, and with John Garang in Juba, who was the head of the south Sudanese revolutionaries. I negotiated back and forth for three days, and finally said I would call a press conference on CNN to announce which one was preventing the eradication of Guinea worm. The result was a two-month ceasefire, to give the Carter Center access, which actually lasted more than six months. We've now completely eliminated Guinea worm from north Sudan – now Sudan – and in South Sudan, it only affects about five villages. They still call the 1995 peace agreement the 'Guinea Worm Ceasefire'.

Is there a case for arguing that presidents are actually more effective when they have left power?

As President of the United States of America, I had thousands of people working for me, I had a powerful military force, I had financial resources that I could use. I don't have those sorts of things now. But what I do have is knowledge of people that I never would have gained had I still been in office. And to see the gratitude on the face of a child who has just been cured of a disease, and the parents who know their child will live. I have a lot more time to go to the areas where need is greatest.

The Carter Center is not constrained by the niceties of diplomacy. I can go where I wish, meet with whom I choose and say what I want. There is always a place for NGOs, and the partnerships we form make it possible for the Carter Center to perform its duties.

The world is witnessing humanitarian crises on an unprecedented scale. How can the international community begin to tackle these problems?

We approached this question after the Second World War. We organised the United Nations hoping we would never have another world war, and that the UN could act effectively in the case of civil war or conflict between two countries. That dream has basically been abandoned. Now, the incapacity of the US, Russia, China, the UK and others to control the UN and cooperate with each other, means that these terrible conflicts evolve. And when conflict evolves in an area, the protection of human rights is gone.

If we could just do what we thought we were doing in the late 1940s – to develop a peaceful world through the UN and the Universal Declaration of Human Rights – we would see great change and great progress. ○

A balancing act

Princess Lamia AlSaud

We live in an era of painful contrasts, where there is more prosperity and also more desperate poverty than ever before. Princess Lamia AlSaud, the head of Alwaleed Philanthropies, explains why more must be done to build a fairer and more sustainable world

———

Princess Lamia AlSaud
Secretary general, Alwaleed Philanthropies

———

THE AUTHOR

Princess Lamia Bint Majed AlSaud
is secretary general of Alwaleed
Philanthropies, a charitable and
philanthropic organisation that
has pledged $32bn towards efforts
to combat poverty, empower
women and youth, develop
communities, provide disaster relief
and create cultural understanding
through education

—

I grew up in a family and a society where I was taught from an early age of my responsibility to those less fortunate than me. My faith, coupled with the example set by my elders, encouraged me to use my talents and education to make a positive contribution to society.

Today I count myself blessed to have that opportunity as secretary general of Alwaleed Philanthropies. For more than 30 years the foundation has provided much-needed emergency relief in the wake of major disasters such as the Nepal earthquake, has helped marginalised communities all over the world, and striven to foster greater cultural understanding.

The vision of our founder Prince Alwaleed Bin Talal AlSaud is to build a fairer and more sustainable world; one in which humanity is not concerned with religious, racial or gender divides. From our earliest days we have been one of the only philanthropic foundations based in the Arab world to have helped people from all over the globe. To date, we have supported thousands of projects in more than 120 countries.

Yet this is just the beginning. In an era of perplexing and painful contrasts, there is always more to do. In many ways our world today is more prosperous and presents greater opportunities than ever before. Yet we also live in a time when far too many have been left behind. Wherever we look, there is hardship and suffering. Hundreds of millions of people remain in the grip of poverty and disease. Families are forced by conflict or natural disaster to flee for their lives. Cultural divisions and misunderstanding pose new threats to safety and stability.

Our global humanitarian system is struggling to cope with the strain, and instead of the unity and cooperation required to put this right, we find divisions and misunderstanding preventing collective action and undermining our shared future.

Within this deeply challenging environment, the role of modern philanthropy is increasingly indispensable. It can move with the urgency that crises demand and take risks and innovate in a way that can be difficult for governments to emulate. This freedom and flexibility enables it to invest in long-term solutions that do more than simply treat symptoms.

In 2016 our founder became the first Muslim Arab to sign the Giving Pledge, promising to dedicate his entire $32bn fortune to help build a world of tolerance, acceptance, equality and opportunity for all. It is now for us to deliver on that generosity. We are determined to step up our mission to combat poverty, empower women and youth, develop communities, provide disaster relief and create cultural understanding through education.

We also recognise that if we are to accelerate progress, we have to find new ways of working together and ways to build new partnerships. The challenges we face in philanthropy today are global in nature and so complex that no single organisation, or single sector, can resolve them. By drawing on the resources and experiences of many stakeholders, we can find more effective and sustainable solutions.

'Tackling gender inequality needs to be placed at the heart of our response to humanitarian crises... Women and children suffer disproportionately in such circumstances'

While providing emergency disaster relief remains central to what we do, we are working to put in place mechanisms that will help humanitarian staff meet needs more effectively and also achieve longer-term development goals. With Save the Children, for example, we are developing 10 rapid response centres to provide frontline humanitarian staff with the latest skills, knowledge and technology to respond faster and more effectively in the event of natural or man-made catastrophes.

We are also putting an even higher priority on lifting the barriers that prevent wider development and prosperity. At a time when human capital is the greatest resource of all, there is no more significant obstacle than gender inequality. We need everyone, no matter what their gender or background, to be able to reach their full potential and make their contribution to progress.

As you might expect from a foundation with an all-female team, this is something about which we feel very strongly. We know reducing gender inequality is one of the most effective ways of driving social and economic progress, and this goal influences every aspect of our work. With our partners, we support and fund initiatives to ensure women have access to education, employment and intellectual freedom. In Saudi Arabia, for example, we support the Wa'iyah Initiative for Women's Legal Rights, which aims to prevent women from becoming victims of violence.

Studies indicate how education provides women with the knowledge and confidence to make their full contribution to society. This is why we also support the Education For Employment initiative that, through locally run organisations across the Middle East and North Africa, helps young women into jobs and on the path to full economic participation.

Tackling gender inequality also needs to be placed at the heart of our response to humanitarian crises. Our experiences in providing emergency relief to victims of conflict and natural disasters have taught us that women and children suffer disproportionately in such circumstances. They have less access to resources and are all too often more vulnerable to threats: sexual abuse, for example, is a real danger for many displaced women and must be taken much more seriously than at present. On a more strategic level, we also need to give women a louder voice in finding long-term solutions to humanitarian problems.

We realise above all that the best route to success is through partnerships. Collaboration between governments, communities, academia, civil society, charitable foundations and other groups can draw on a vast well of knowledge and help to improve our world in a way that is truly global in scale and approach. In this spirit we have provided more than $70m in funding to academic centres, including Harvard and Cambridge universities and the American universities in Beirut and Cairo, to encourage cultural dialogue and tolerance.

'Philanthropy can move with the urgency that crises demand and take risks and innovate in a way that can be difficult for governments'

As a team we are immensely proud of the work we have done and are excited about the potential for the future. Through our passion and by partnering with each other, we have the opportunity to accelerate global change and shape our world for the better. I feel blessed to be part of this cause, and invite everyone to join us on this journey towards equity and fairness for all. ○

"The challenges we
face in philanthropy today
are global in nature and so
complex that no
one organisation can
solve them"

Princess Lamia AlSaud

Prescription for change

Kiran Mazumdar-Shaw

For billions of people around the world access to lifesaving drugs depends on where you live and the money in your wallet, rather than medical need. Kiran Mazumdar-Shaw explains why we need innovation in the pharmaceutical industry to make sure we care for everyone, at all times and in all places

———————

Kiran Mazumdar-Shaw
Managing director, Biocon

————

THE AUTHOR

Kiran Mazumdar-Shaw is
chairperson and managing
director of Biocon, India's largest
biotech company, which she
founded in 1978. The company's
associated Biocon Foundation
aims to promote social and
economic inclusion by helping
marginalised communities access
healthcare and education

————

I t is an ugly truth that in the eyes of multinational pharma firms, the wealthy, western patient – and profit – comes first. It is a practice South African health minister, Aaron Motsoaledi, condemned in January 2014 when he said big pharmaceutical companies would be sentencing people in developing countries to "death" with a campaign to effectively scotch access to generic drugs. "I am not using strong words; I am using appropriate words. This is genocide," he said.

His comments created a stir, but his ire pointed to the seriousness of the issue: that the current western pharmaceutical model doesn't work for poorer people. Its restrictive patent regimes sustain superlative profits, which discriminate against patients on the basis of nationality, race and economic status. It is a model that ends up putting a price on life by putting a price on lifesaving drugs. It is no surprise then that nearly 2 billion people – or a third of the world's population – lack access to essential medicines.

No more was this apparent than during the outbreak of the deadly Ebola virus in West Africa in 2014. As Ebola surfaces sporadically in low-income, African countries, multinational pharma corporations see little incentive to invest in a vaccine. Poor Africans died even though the world had access to the science for a drug to fend off Ebola. Media reports indicated promise in Ebola vaccine trials. But this piece of good news came too late for the more than 11,000 people who died of the disease, a majority of them in the poorest nations such as Guinea, Liberia and Sierra Leone.

The Ebola crisis has echoes of the 1990s AIDS epidemic, when millions of poor Africans were dying for lack of affordable medicines. While patients in the US could afford HIV/ AIDS drugs of $12,000 per patient per year, they were clearly beyond the reach of those in Africa. The world seemed to accept the unacceptable, until in 2001 an Indian pharmaceutical company produced a three-in-one HIV/AIDS treatment for $1 a day.

Affordability is the key to accessibility. In the economic reality of a developing country, cheaper drugs and low-priced healthcare infrastructure models can work wonders. Today, most of the antiretroviral medicines purchased by the US' global AIDS programme and more than 80 per cent of the HIV drugs used by Médecins Sans Frontières, UNICEF and the Clinton Foundation are generics from India. We only need look at the hope that cheaper generics have brought to Africa's AIDS victims to realise the transformative potential of affordability.

India has emerged as a pharmacy to the world thanks to an intellectual property environment that fosters cheaper drug innovation – an environment that respects patents but counters the continuation of monopolistic markets.

In addition to antiretrovirals, generic producers in India have brought down the prices of lifesaving drugs used to treat killer diseases such as TB, cancer and diabetes by as much as 90 per cent. In doing so, India has emerged as a vital producer of affordable medicines and the world's largest producer of generic drugs. Today, the Indian pharmaceutical industry accounts for 20 per cent of the world's pharma industry in value terms, and constitutes a significant 80 per cent in volume terms.

Still, the country cannot single-handedly address the global need for affordable medicines and affordability is not simple to implement. It requires creative thinking. Thus to deliver affordability, we require innovation; innovation in discovering drugs, developing therapeutics and delivering healthcare. It is only by creating innovation in technology, strategies, practices and policies that we can take on the global healthcare challenges that we face.

Some of this innovation can come from the private sector. I started Biocon driven by the desire to create a business that would leverage science for the benefit of society through affordable innovation. When we began we had a choice to develop low-cost generic pharmaceuticals or complex, capital-intensive premium products. We chose the latter. Through innovative process engineering, we found we could deliver affordable pricing and make a difference to global healthcare. We made long-term investments in creating complex biologics manufacturing capabilities and commissioned operations in locations where we could leverage the advantages of cost, scale and knowledge to bring prices down. Over time, we successfully developed advanced biopharmaceuticals against diabetes and cancer – previously available only in the west – to patients in India and other developing countries at price points that made them affordable and accessible.

'In the economic reality of a developing country, cheaper drugs and low-priced healthcare infrastructure models can work wonders'

Innovation, too, is needed in the way healthcare is delivered. We can make a difference, for example, through community-based prevention programmes for diabetes, oral cancer, cervical cancer and hypertension that focus on education and early detection through community screening. ICT-based ehealthcare also holds much promise, for example using such technology to gather data to spot the gaps in quality healthcare for underserved communities, and helping the healthcare sector plan more effectively. Our foundation is starting to develop ehealthcare's potential, which would add to Biocon Foundation's programmes on health insurance, health delivery and health education, which touch the lives of almost 500,000 people each year.

I believe the pharmaceutical industry has a humanitarian responsibility to provide affordable access to essential drugs for patients who are in need, and to do so with the power of innovation. I believe the healthcare industry has a special responsibility as we sell essential life-enhancing and lifesaving medicines and provide life-giving care. We cannot profit at the cost of patients.

We are starting to see a change. Big pharma is beginning to notice that global priorities are shifting from providing exclusive and expensive drugs to more affordable, accessible medicines. This goes hand-in-hand with the realisation that the opportunities are in emerging markets; this reality is already compelling several multinational pharmaceutical companies to introduce differential pricing in emerging markets.

It is time to create a new paradigm to address the escalating crisis in global healthcare. We must ensure those who need lifesaving medicines get it, at all times and in all places. o

"Affordability is the key to accessibility. We cannot profit at the cost of patients"

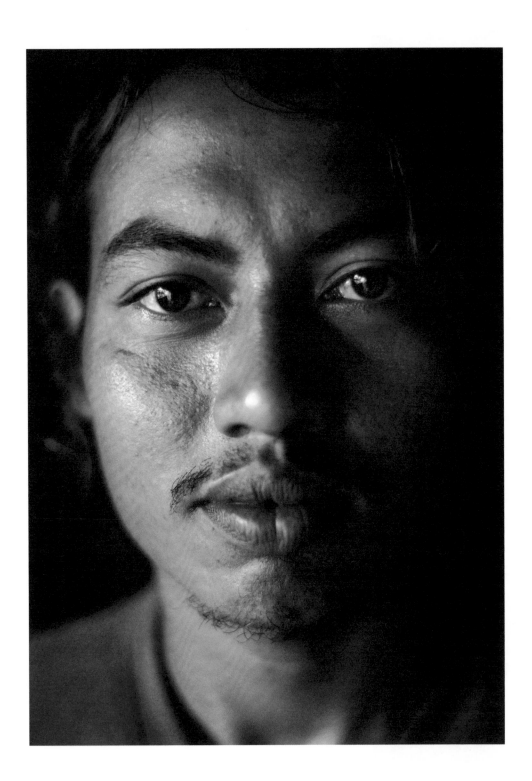

Blood money

Nick Grono

Slavery is a $150bn industry built on the misery and suffering of human beings. Nick Grono, CEO of the Freedom Fund, argues that with more people championing the anti-slavery fight we can – and must – do more to help the estimated 46 million men, women and children enslaved around the world today

Nick Grono
CEO, Freedom Fund

———

THE AUTHOR

Nick Grono is CEO of the Freedom Fund, the world's first private donor fund dedicated to tackling slavery around the world. Previously, he worked at conflict resolution NGO the International Crisis Group, and at the Walk Free Foundation where he helped to launch the first Global Slavery Index, now produced annually

——

S lavery has been with us for millennia, documented in records scratched on 4,000-year-old tablets. Yet, while it would be comforting to think that slavery is a relic of history, sadly that is not the case. Despite the powerful work of past abolitionists, it still exists in every country in the world, and thrives in many.

Although slavery is prohibited everywhere, an estimated 46 million people globally are enslaved today. The essence of this horrific crime is the control of individuals through violence and other forms of coercion, to force them to work. .

Modern-day slavery touches all of us. Our mobile phones contain minerals often sourced from Congolese mines, where children labour under the control of militias. Our supermarket shelves are likely stocked with cheap prawns and fish from Thailand, produced by Burmese and Cambodian migrants enslaved on Thai fishing boats. Our cheap clothing may have been manufactured by girls in bondage in Bangladesh, or made from cotton produced by forced labour in Uzbekistan. And in our cities, vulnerable girls and women in search of better lives have likely been deceived and forced to work in brothels, subject to rape on a nightly basis.

But why is slavery so prevalent, given that it is prohibited in every country? Modern slavery thrives when three factors intersect: the demand for extremely cheap labour, individual vulnerability and marginalisation, and weak rule of law.

Slavery is fuelled by the demand for extremely cheap labour. Of course, there is nothing legally wrong with seeking lower labour costs, as long as this is done in compliance with the law. But when it comes to modern slavery, the objective is to pay excessively low wages, invariably in breach of that law. Sadly, there is often a compelling economic case for slavery – for the perpetrator. It allows

"It's shameful that slavery still exists in the 21st century. But I believe that, together, we can end this crime against humanity"

———

businesses to minimise their labour costs illicitly, producing ever-cheaper goods and services while maximising profits. According to the International Labour Organisation, annual profits from slavery amount to $150bn.

The demand for cheap inputs is also driven by our globalised economy, with supply chains often spanning continents. Multinationals may have five or six layers in their supply chains: from the high-street retailer all the way back to the cotton picker in Uzbekistan, or the fisherman in Thailand, or the artisanal miner in the Congo. At each layer there is pressure to reduce costs further, so we consumers can get our $3 t-shirts, or cheap sushi, or ever-faster smartphones.

Of course, the demand for cheap labour does not enable slavery on its own. Slavery requires vulnerable human beings, who can be tricked or coerced into exploitative situations, as well as a failure to hold those breaking the law accountable for their crimes.

Vulnerability often takes the form of poverty. Poverty alone is not a determinant of slavery: many poor countries and regions are not disproportionately afflicted with slavery. But where you have poverty combined with a lack of economic alternatives, people take risks in the quest for a better life.

It causes people to engage in risky migration, enabling criminals and traffickers to take advantage of their desire for a better future.

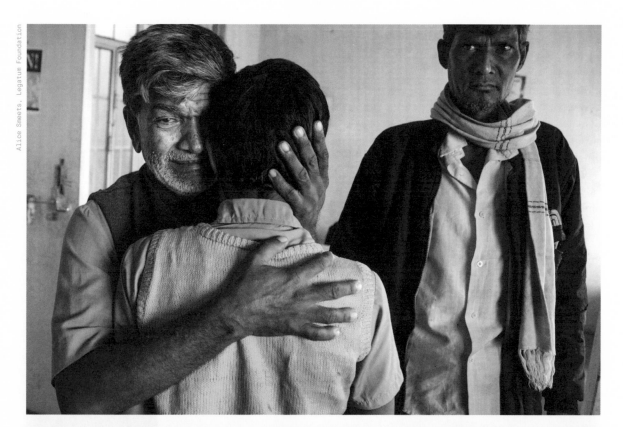

Alice Smeets, Legatum Foundation

Sanjit Das, Legatum Foundation

Young women from Ukraine or Moldova, for example, are often deceived by promises of better lives in western countries. Despite having heard stories of the risks of sex trafficking, they migrate anyway, hoping the horror stories won't happen to them.

Vulnerability takes many other forms such as conflict and displacement, caste, ethnicity, gender, illiteracy, and migrant status, usually combined with societal discrimination against the differentiating trait.

Migrants and refugees are particularly vulnerable. Syrian refugees are now being exploited heavily in the fields of Lebanon and factories of Turkey, given their desperate need to work – often illegally – to survive.

Finally, we have the rule of law. Modern slavery is prohibited under international law, and illegal everywhere. Modern slavery is also morally repugnant. So the fact that slavery exists on the scale it does, means that there is a fundamental failure in implementing the law, and in internalising the norms against slavery and extreme exploitation. Modern slavery thrives under weak rule of law and bad governance. It is enabled by corruption, and practised by abusive power-holders.

Whole communities in South Asia are openly enslaved through debt bondage and forced to work in brick kilns or stone quarries, which are often owned by local criminal or political figures, and given protection by officials. The massive red light districts in India's big cities are a vacuum for trafficked minors: brothels there thrive because of police and bureaucratic indifference at best, and co-option at worst.

Conflict-ridden countries and those with weak institutions are at particular risk of exposing their citizens to a heightened risk of slavery, along with many other evils. Think of child soldiers in Central Africa, the sexual slavery of girls and women practised by ISIS and Boko Haram, and the use of forced labour by rebels and government militias alike to extract conflict minerals.

All of this makes fighting modern slavery a daunting task, as it means confronting powerful economic models, and entrenched discrimination and corruption. That's no mean feat.

Yet there are reasons for optimism. First, political and religious leaders are increasingly championing the fight. US President Barack Obama has long been a vocal advocate of anti-slavery efforts. UK Prime Minister Theresa May has declared slavery "the great human rights issue of our time" and affirmed her commitment "to rid our world of this barbaric evil". India, home to an estimated 18 million people in slavery, has introduced new legislation to combat sex and labour trafficking. And Pope Francis is a highly visible and vocal proponent of efforts to combat slavery and exploitation.

Businesses are also becoming more aware of the presence of slavery in their supply chains. Transparency legislation in the UK

Alice Smeets, Legatum Foundation

'Fighting modern slavery is a daunting task. It means confronting powerful economic models, and discrimination and corruption'

and California, and reputational risk, is encouraging them to take action beyond superficial declarations of intent.

We are beginning to see increased interest by funders in support of efforts to tackle and eliminate slavery. Given the relative paucity of resources currently devoted to fight this $150bn global, criminal industry, that's a welcome development – and yet we still have a long way to go.

There has been an explosion of investigative journalism into slavery, led by the Guardian, Thomson Reuters, Associated Press, the New York Times, Al Jazeera and others. This media increases the awareness of consumers, and pressures businesses and governments to do better.

New advances in technology are driving greater transparency. Technology allows us to be connected to the people and stories behind our products in ways that were never possible before. It drives better communication, allowing organisations and companies to listen to workers and help them to better express their rights.

Finally, all of these developments are contributing to consumers becoming more aware of slavery and its role in producing products like mobile phones, fast fashion and low-cost seafood. Consumers have the power to demand that brands and their suppliers do better, and that is an important lever for change.

It's shameful that slavery still exists in the 21st century and that every country is besmirched by this evil. But I believe that, together, we can end this crime against humanity. I invite you to join in this growing global anti-slavery movement so that we can complete the work of those abolitionists who have gone before us, and end the nightmare of slavery once and for all. ○

Upwardly mobile

Judith Rodin

Solving the world's problems requires greater financial muscle than
governments, aid agencies and philanthropists can muster. After
pioneering impact investing to mobilise the private sector, Judith Rodin
explains how we need to put the innovation back into innovative finance
to help more people do good

———

Judith Rodin

President, Rockefeller Foundation

————

THE AUTHOR

Judith Rodin is president of the Rockefeller Foundation, established in 1913. Today, the foundation aims to build greater resilience and advance more inclusive economies. Prior to joining the foundation in 2005, Rodin was president of the University of Pennsylvania and provost of Yale University

——

W hen Shaffi Mather's mother was found choking in her sleep
in Kerala, India, there wasn't a local ambulance he could call
to get her the emergency care she needed. His mother survived, but
Shaffi couldn't shake the idea that he could do something to solve
this problem for others in the community. Together with friends he
launched an emergency medical service, Dial 1298 for Ambulance,
modelled after the 911 number in the United States.

They set up a new company, Ziqitza Health Care Limited (ZHL),
with support from the London Ambulance Service, but Mather and
his cofounders knew they would need to find a sustainable source
of funding to keep the initiative going. They developed a business
model that allows patients to pay for services on a sliding scale
based on the hospital they can afford. The founders also attracted
additional financing from philanthropies, commercial investors and
government contracts. As of 2013, ZHL had a turnover of $20m and
has saved the lives of more than 4,000 Mumbai residents.

ZHL is an outstanding example of the potential for impact when
actors from all sectors come together to finance social needs. But
we need many more like ZHL if we are going to fill the gap between
the world's problems and the amount of money available to solve
them. The funding gap for the new UN Sustainable Development
Goals alone is approximately $2.5 trillion annually – and that's just
in developing countries. Governments, development agencies and
philanthropy only have billions available to spend.

Fortunately, both investors and businesses alike are seeing
the benefits of moving beyond short-termism to generate
both a profit and positive social or environmental impact.
For one, we're seeing a generational shift in that direction: more than
92 per cent of millennials believe that a business' purpose extends

beyond profit and this generation stands to inherit more than $30 trillion of intergenerational wealth – and associated investment decisions – in the next few decades. For another, businesses are starting to see that advancing more inclusive economies is improving not only the lives of employees, customers and potential customers, but it can boost the bottom line too. Finally, we see more entrepreneurial people like Shaffi who are taking it upon themselves to find business solutions to social and environmental problems.

At the Rockefeller Foundation we saw the opportunity to leverage these trends to bring greater financial resources to bear on global challenges. In 2007, we brought together social, finance and philanthropic leaders who coined the term "impact investing" to define investments made with the intention of creating both financial return and social or environmental impact.

As a result of these efforts, socially-responsible assets under management doubled to more than $60bn between 2012 and 2014, and three-quarters of participants in the 2015 JP Morgan/Global Impact Investing Network impact investor survey reported that their portfolios are performing to financial expectations while simultaneously delivering satisfactory impact. While capital allocation is still heavily tilted towards North America, 51 per cent of assets under management are in emerging markets.

Despite the amount of private capital that impact investing has mobilised, it is still not enough to solve all the problems the world faces. We need additional mechanisms to mobilise more capital from more sources that help people do good; not just as humanitarians but as investors.

To do this, we need to put the innovation back into innovative finance. That's exactly what we are working towards through Zero Gap, which looks to develop the next generation of innovative finance partnerships, processes and platforms. Employing a venture philanthropy model, Zero Gap supports early-stage design and experimentation with both private and public sector partners. This work is focused on solutions that can ultimately catalyse large-scale capital from institutional investors, as well as households and retail investors, to benefit poor and vulnerable people. Zero Gap mechanisms under exploration include micro-levies – which are micro-taxes on individual transactions of global industries, such as air travel – to raise large-scale funding. Other models leverage public credit to attract and crowd-in more resources from the private sector.

We are also looking at how we might improve the 'pay-for-success' model that is behind the rise of social impact bonds. For example, we are working with Yunus Social Business to develop a social success note. Through this instrument, an investor agrees to make a concessional loan to a social business, which the social business must pay back.

'There is still not enough private capital mobilised today to solve all the problems the world faces'

The twist is that if the social business hits a predetermined social impact target, the philanthropic donor will pay the investor an additional amount for the social impact achieved which would otherwise not have been possible but for that initial investment in the social business. Lower risk, higher reward, means that more investors may look to social businesses like Dial 1298 for Ambulance to bring more market-based solutions to developing nations, while getting a financial return.

In addition to attracting more money to solve social and environmental problems, innovative finance can help to spread risk

"We believe innovative finance is the next frontier of what it means to do well by doing good"

Judith Rodin

from severe events among private and public markets. For example, Africa Risk Capacity's Extreme Climate Facility is working to make more private and international funding available to eligible African countries to help them build climate resilience and be financially prepared to undertake greater adaptation measures, with extreme weather events increasing in frequency and intensity in the region.

We believe innovative finance is the next frontier of what it means to do well by doing good, and emerging markets in particular have a great deal to gain from this shift.

But most critically, we're learning that in this century, you can't do good – or enough good – on your own. We need to work together across sectors: philanthropy has the expertise and the risk capital; business has the scope and scale; and governments make the policies and incentives. And it is this cross-sectoral collaboration, as the people who have made it to hospital because of Dial 1298 for Ambulance show us, that can make a lifesaving and world-changing difference. ○

'We're learning that in this century, you can't do good – or enough good – on your own'

Great expectations

Melinda Gates is one half of the world's most generous private philanthropic organisation: the Bill & Melinda Gates Foundation. Here, she shares her thoughts on female empowerment, impactful philanthropy and why the learning never stops on her own giving journey

————

Melinda Gates is co-chair of the Bill & Melinda Gates Foundation. Along with her husband, Bill, she shapes and approves the foundation's strategies and overall direction, to further the organisation's goal of improving equity in the US and around the world.

What was your goal for the Gates Foundation when it launched in 2000?

The work we do is grounded in the principle that every life has equal value. We were inspired to act after reading a newspaper article about rotavirus, a diarrhoeal disease that was killing about half a million children in developing countries each year. We were shocked to learn that while most children get it, for the most part only children in poor countries were dying from it. This motivated us to use our resources to accelerate development of a vaccine to protect children everywhere, and that led us to get more deeply involved in some of the other problems that face people living in extreme poverty.

In terms of impact, we're a large foundation, but even our resources can't begin to solve the world's biggest challenges. Almost everything we do is in conjunction with partners in government, the private sector, and civil society – whether it's delivering lifesaving vaccines to children, ensuring that women have access to contraceptives, or tackling the world's biggest killer diseases: HIV, tuberculosis and malaria.

How does private philanthropy differ from aid?

Each has a role to play, but they complement each other – and, more than that, they rely on each other. In 2013, countries around the world contributed more than $150bn in development assistance: that's 60 times the average annual budget of our foundation. In our view, the role of private foundations is to operate as a catalyst to accelerate impact. We can't match the giving capacity of governments, but we have more flexibility to take risks, knowing some ideas may fail.

How do you set your giving priorities?

As Bill has said before, we don't have any kind of magic formula for prioritising the world's problems. But we knew we wanted to invest in areas where we could have the greatest impact on the most number of people. So we looked for issues where a relatively small investment could spur meaningful and sustainable progress – accelerating the development of a rotavirus vaccine, for example. Data also helps us to set priorities. We spend a lot of time in developing countries to help us understand more about what life is like for the people who live there. We need to be out in the field, meeting people and letting their real life experiences shape our work.

You are a vocal advocate for female empowerment. Why are women and girls so critical to the success of global development goals?

There are a number of reasons why, but here's one of the most important: if a woman has a dollar in her pocket, she uses about eighty cents of that to provide for her family, purchasing things like healthy food, doctor visits and education. I talk to women about finances quite a bit. Almost universally, one of the first priorities they mention is their children's school. Whether they talk about books, fees, or supplies, it's the first thing on their minds.

Their investments pay off. When mothers decide how their families' money is spent, their children are 20 per cent more likely to survive, and much more likely to thrive. Focusing on women and girls is the most direct way to ensure healthier and more prosperous families, and greater economic progress around the world.

What more can be done to help shift the paradigm for women and girls in developing countries?

As I've taught my three children, it's crucial that those of us who do have a voice use it to speak up for the women and girls who don't. It's our responsibility to advocate for women and girls everywhere to ensure that they grow up healthy and respected, and able to create a better future for themselves and their families. We are not there yet. Every single day, 800 women die in childbirth, mostly of preventable causes. That's unacceptable, and the world needs to do more to address it. More voices, more support, more education, more collaboration – these are just a few of the actions anyone reading this can take right now.

When you reflect on the work you've done over the years, what are you most proud of?

We are very proud to be part of GAVI, the vaccine alliance. GAVI coordinates efforts between businesses, governments, and aid agencies to deliver lifesaving vaccines to children in poor countries who need them most. So far, GAVI has enabled more than 500 million children to be vaccinated, saving more than 7 million lives.

Another important moment for me was helping organise a family planning summit in London in 2012. Dozens of countries came together to commit to helping more than 100 million women get access to the contraceptives they want to plan and space their pregnancies. The effort raised more than $2bn, the first time the world put a 'b' in front of a fundraising effort for women and girls. That's something I'll never forget.

What advice would you give to would-be philanthropists at the start of their giving journey?

Look for a problem that markets and governments aren't paying much attention to. Find something that moves you that not many people are working on, and start learning about it. There are no shortage of problems calling out for attention, compassion and solutions.

Then, keep learning. That never stops. You have to be talking constantly to experts and partners and using the data to help you evaluate honestly what has worked and what hasn't. And also understand that you can't do it alone. You need partners who share your vision, but also offer complementary skills, experience and knowledge.

The motto of my high school in Texas was *'serviam',* which means 'I will serve'. That's something I've always taken very seriously. It's not so much advice as it is a reminder that we're here on this planet to use our resources and abilities to lift up those around us.

With the benefit of hindsight, what would your current self tell the couple who started the foundation?

The years since we launched have been an incredible learning journey. Because Bill and I both come from a technology background, we had a natural bias towards technological solutions, like vaccines or higher-yielding seeds for farmers. And while those are important – essential, even – we've also learned that designing a solution that makes sense in the daily realities of people's lives is as important as the technology itself to broader success. You really have to understand the context of the culture in which you're operating, to have an impact.

I'd also want to reassure us that incredible progress is possible. You can't solve problems like newborn mortality or extreme poverty overnight. And sometimes, the pace of change can be frustrating. But we believe the years to 2030 will unlock the fastest progress for people living in extreme poverty that the world has ever seen. It's going to be an exciting thing to be a part of. I'd urge you to get involved. ○

Food of the future

Mark Post

Man's carnivorous tendencies are putting the planet under pressure. With the twin challenges of how to feed a growing world population and reduce the environmental impact of food production, Mark Post examines one of the technological solutions to satiate our growing appetite for meat – by growing it in a lab

———

Mark Post
Professor, Maastricht University

––––––––

THE AUTHOR

Mark Post is professor of
vascular physiology at Maastricht
University, the Netherlands.
He first became involved in
investigating 'in vitro meat' in
2008, as professor of tissue
engineering. In 2013, he and
his team grew the world's first
synthetic hamburger from
cultured beef cells

––

Humans have come a long way in 15,000 years. Then, we were only just able to feed ourselves and perhaps some family or tribe members by hunting and gathering food. Yet innovation in agriculture, including the domestication and selective breeding of animals, made food production vastly more efficient and enabled the enormous expansion of our civilisation.

Food productivity is still increasing, which allows the growth of humans on this planet to continue its march towards a projected 9.7 billion people by 2050. The parallel expansion of global wealth has led to a drastic change in eating habits: we consume more and more so-called 'high quality' proteins from meat. Indeed, the World Health Organisation estimates that our consumption of meat will rise by 70 per cent in the coming three decades.

If this prediction turns out to be true, we will reach the limit of current agricultural systems – the availability of land, water, energy and capacity to absorb greenhouse gases – before we achieve full food security. Already, 70 per cent of arable land is taken up by livestock meat production.

We can increase production by either recruiting more land, or by improving productivity. Using up more land is environmentally very costly. With animals such as cows that breed slowly and in small litter sizes, it is hard and time consuming – if possible at all – to boost productivity. Cows in particular are the least efficient producers of meat: for every pound of beef, the cow eats up to 10 pounds of feed. Since a large proportion of feed consists of grains and soy that can serve as a protein source for humans as well, we lose a tremendous amount of nutrients by feeding cows. It is a tenacious myth that we need animal proteins to survive. Voluntary vegetarians in meat-eating societies and involuntary vegetarians in

developing economies prove otherwise. Yet we continue to eat meat. As omnivores, our digestive and metabolic system is geared towards vegetable and meat intake, a function that has contributed to our evolutionary success. Still, even if the evolutionary and biological drivers of dietary behaviour are poorly understood, what is clear is that turning all humans into herbivores is not the solution. We must find other ways to satiate our desire for meat.

In a 1931 essay titled 'Fifty Years Hence' Winston Churchill, later British prime minister, wrote: "Fifty years hence, we shall escape the absurdity of growing a whole chicken in order to eat the breast or wing, by growing these parts separately under a suitable medium." Some 80 years later, the identification of the muscle-specific stem cell, the so-called satellite cell, made lab-grown meat a reality. The first proof of principle in the form of a beef hamburger – completely cultured from satellite cells – was unveiled, cooked and eaten in 2013. Produced at the scale we think is achievable and cost effective, laboratory-cultured meat could cost about $65 per kilo. The biggest driver of cost is the amount of cells you can culture per millilitre of fluid. Our calculations are based on the assumption of growing 5 million cells per millilitre; but some of the bioreactors out there have already reported numbers much higher than that. If that number increases ten-fold, the price will come down ten-fold. This technology could be used to produce any meat, fish or chicken.

Cost is not the only challenge to a cultured-meat future. There is an emotional aversion towards food grown in a laboratory. It is unknown how widespread or persistent these reservations are. For sure, there will be major regional and cultural differences in acceptance of highly technological foods. But our survey from a sample of people in western Europe found that up to 60 per cent would be in favour of this technology, while 50 per cent were willing to buy and eat cultured beef. Safety concerns and its seemingly unnatural quality are also typically among the factors mentioned by the general public. But cultured meat will eventually be exactly the same as the animal tissue we presently consume, so it will be safe and arguably safer than what we rear and eat now – we currently have limited control over contamination and disease, whereas a cultured system can provide that assurance. These elements make me hopeful this technology will be adopted.

I believe the uptake of lab-grown meat would start in industrialised countries in western Europe or the US. The rich part of the world can afford to indulge in a more expensive product that relieves our consciences of meat's environmental and ethical impact. If we are capable of producing exactly the same product as livestock-produced beef at a competitive price everyone can afford and at scale, cultured meat will spread gradually to the rest of the world. When it becomes the norm, then we will be able to make the global difference we really seek.

'In a 1931 essay Winston Churchill wrote: "Fifty years hence, we shall escape the absurdity of growing a whole chicken to eat the breast or wing"'

———

In my mind, by 2050, the entirety of the world's population could be fed by cultured meat. In reality, I don't know how long it will take, but I believe there can only be one scenario – and that's a total shift to cultured meat production. This is not because people won't want to eat livestock-produced beef or other meats, but simply because we eventually won't have that choice. The imperative to secure food for the global population must be balanced with the need to reduce humans' environmental pressure on the planet.

Providing food for 9.7 billion people in an environmentally friendly and ethical way is a formidable task that requires all the ingenuity we can muster. Technological solutions are on the horizon – including food waste reduction, improvement of plant-based meat substitutes, insect proteins and, of course, cultured meat. A multi-level, multi-target approach has the best chance of redesigning our food future in such a way that our choices respect the boundaries of humanity and the environment. Lab-grown meat can be a part of that mix. o

'The imperative of food security must be balanced with the need to reduce humans' environmental pressure on the planet'

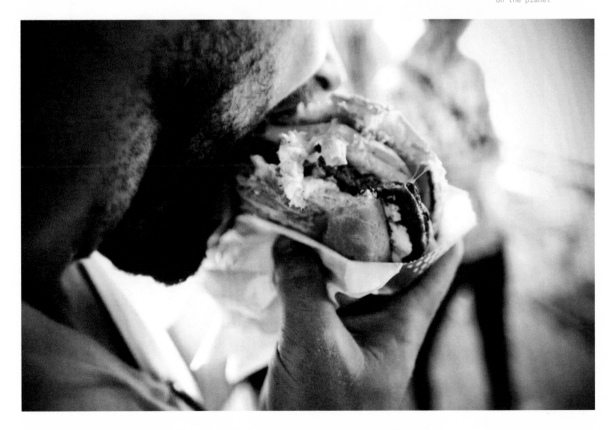

Empowering a generation

Ron Bruder

Unlocking the economic potential of women could be
transformative for the Middle East and North Africa, its
governments and, crucially, for the dignity and empowerment
of the individuals themselves. Ron Bruder explains why it's in
all our interests to enable women to work and earn

Ron Bruder
Founder, Education For Employment

———

THE AUTHOR

Ron Bruder is a serial entrepreneur and philanthropist. He founded, and seed-funded, Education For Employment (EFE), the Middle East and North Africa's leading youth employment nonprofit network. EFE works to provide market-driven skills to unemployed young women and men, and link them to jobs

———

G rowing up, Montaha Abu Libdeh and her nine brothers and sisters faced hardships sadly all-too common among the embattled citizens of Gaza, Palestine. Their father was sick and unable to work, their mother bent double under the pressure of supporting such a large family. Two siblings died during an ill-fated protest. "These circumstances pushed me to become a positive actor in my family's journey of survival," Montaha says. "To become that, I needed to find a job."

Montaha had a university degree, but she faced a challenge familiar to millions of women across the Middle East and North Africa (MENA): that of developing a skillset appropriate to the needs of employers in the region – and then rising above significant historical, cultural and circumstantial barriers to find employment. She found her path in a training programme run by the Palestine branch of Education For Employment (EFE), which enabled her to transform an internship at a local engineering consultancy into a full-time position. Today, she is a talented young architect with the same firm, hoping to rebuild what has been razed, and helping every day to support her family.

Montaha's story is a positive one, but one which cannot cloud the reality that for too long, women have been without their proper place in the labour market in MENA. Female labour force participation in the region is just 23 per cent, the lowest in the world. It's an imbalance that is stymying growth and opportunity for millions. At the same time, were we to address and overcome this disparity, we would find ourselves entering an era that could prove transformational for the region, its peoples and its governments. The economic argument alone is overwhelming: McKinsey reports that full equality in labour markets in MENA could boost regional

GDP by 47 per cent over the next ten years, and that the region could realise $600bn in economic impact annually, or $2.7 trillion by 2025. The World Bank notes that raising female employment to male levels would, for example, boost GDP in Egypt and the UAE by 34 per cent and 12 per cent, respectively.

At EFE, we have decided that facilitating the transition of young women into the labour force or into self-employment is a particular priority. We are proud that more than 53 per cent of EFE graduates are female. We have placed more than 4,000 young women into jobs, and provided thousands more with the skills they need to pursue their own pathways to employment or start their own microenterprises.

On a personal level, I would like to see young women's employment continue as a major focus for us. Overcoming social stereotypes is a key challenge that we continue to face. Particularly in the early days of EFE, we would often train a young woman and get her ready for a job, only to have her family decide that they did not want her working. As an organisation, we are still grappling with this obstacle, and have developed specialised tactics and programmes to deal with these situations – from bringing families to worksites so they can see the conditions for themselves, to launching the first region-wide survey of young women and employers aimed at identifying the specific barriers to young women's employment, and proposing steps for overcoming them.

One of the gamechangers in overcoming obstacles to young women's employment is finding the right employer partners. Nearly 2,000 companies have hired EFE alumni, and many of them recognise the dual benefit – both to the business and societal – to engaging young women employees. Maliban Factory in Al Shouneh, Jordan, is a long-time employer partner of Jordan EFE and a great example of a company that is doing well by doing good. The factory operates in one of the most economically depressed and conservative areas of Jordan, yet more than 95 per cent of its staff are young women. Why? Because the factory has adopted simple approaches that create a more hospitable environment for female employees – things such as transportation to and from work, for instance – and this puts both the young women employees and their families at ease.

When you speak with Mohammad Qtaishat, who manages the factory, he is very clear on the business benefits of hiring young women: they're better machine operators, and more attentive to detail. But you also see in his eyes that it is about more than making a profit. He has seen that a job in the factory opens a new world to young women who are the first in their families to work. We need more employers like this. First and foremost, women's employment is about personal empowerment, independence and dignity. It is about ensuring that both young women and young men have an

'Overcoming the disparity in female labour force participation could prove transformational for the region'

opportunity to shape their futures, and the financial means to deliver on their dreams.

We all recognise that women's employment also goes beyond individual impact. When a woman becomes a breadwinner her status within the family changes in amazing and important ways. We have seen our alumnae support their mothers and fathers; we have seen them pay for the education of their siblings, or purchase their family's first computer. The more EFE and similar organisations can link young women to work, the more acceptable it becomes in the communities where we operate, and the more role models exist for other young women as they approach working age.

In June 2014, Montaha's house was demolished by the air strikes that flattened much of Gaza to rubble that summer. Her family was forced into rented accommodation: uprooted but unbowed, taking strength from each other and surviving in large part thanks to the income Montaha brings home. "Without having a secure job, I would not have been able to support my family in withstanding these circumstances," she says. "It makes me proud to be a positive agent of support in my family's life."

There are millions more young women with the potential to emulate Montaha, millions more positive agents ready to progress and provide. We need to help them into the world of work, and to support them when they've arrived, so that they may support themselves and others. ○

Guiding light

Forest Whitaker

Actor, filmmaker and humanitarian Forest Whitaker was raised
on the streets of South Central Los Angeles. Today he uses that
experience, and the lessons he learned, to help lift the lives of young
people touched by conflict – and help troubled youth to ignite a fire
bright enough to drive out any darkness

Forest Whitaker
Artist, founder WPDI

THE AUTHOR

An acclaimed actor, director and
producer, Forest Whitaker is the
founder and CEO of the Whitaker
Peace & Development Initiative,
cofounder of the International
Institute for Peace, UNESCO
special envoy for Peace and
Reconciliation, and a member of
the UN Sustainable Development
Goals Advocacy Group

T here is a divine spark within every human being that gives all of us the capacity for extraordinary goodness: to love, to create, to help, to forgive. It is a universal light that connects all of us to the flame of humanity. My journey – as an artist, as an actor, and as a social activist – has always been fundamentally about strengthening my connection with the individual or the character in front of me, to pull away all the outer layers that obscure the truth, and to discover the light hidden deep within.

This search for the light has guided my work from the beginning, as it guides us all. Since I was young, I have had role models who have helped me learn to discover this light where others might overlook it. My mother was a special education teacher who worked closely with students with severe learning disabilities. Watching her interact with those students, seeing the love and attention she gave to each and every one, had a big impact on me. Sometimes I had the opportunity to come to her class and work with these students myself, and I was able to see the strength they possessed as they struggled to cope with some of their challenges.

I saw this light in other hidden places, too. My childhood was marked, in many ways, by conflict. I grew up in South Central Los Angeles during what was a tumultuous time for that part of the city, to say the least. The Watts riots occurred a few miles from my house. The Black Panthers had a headquarters in my neighbourhood that I saw blown up one day by the police. The Bloods and the Crips were formed when I was still a student in middle school.

I had a unique perspective on many of these events, observing them from the inside. Where other people saw controversy and violence, we saw organisations that were trying to help our communities. The Black Panthers were creating lunch programmes and taking care of young kids in our neighbourhood. They would pick me up every day from school and talk to me about taking care of myself and working hard to get an education. Even the Crips and the Bloods started as community-building organisations. Over time, they became criminal groups that waged wholesale violence, but that wasn't the intention of the people who started them; they were giving young people who had been disenfranchised and totally displaced by society a community of their own. I think it's important to understand gangs – to understand all conflict – in this light, to see that conflict and violence are almost always symptoms of some fundamental underlying need that is going unmet. The many friends I had growing up who joined gangs had, in some respects,

been left behind by society. Most came from broken homes, had no real economic opportunities, had no identities. For them, the Crips and the Bloods would become their families. It was devastating to see these destructive forces take over my friends' lives, but I never stopped seeing the light inside them.

I observed something similar many years later when I began working with former child soldiers. It was horrifying to hear these brave young men and women describe their experiences. They had invariably been abused, demoralised, or forced to commit unspeakable acts against their friends and neighbours. Their plights were tragic. But in an insidious way, for many of these youth – even those who had been abducted – being in an armed group filled a need that had been going unmet in their lives. These groups provided many of the youth with food and shelter that they often could not receive elsewhere. Having a role in these groups gave many of these young people a purpose and an identity; a profoundly harmful and destructive one, but an identity nonetheless.

'My childhood was marked by conflict. I grew up in South Central Los Angeles during what was a tumultuous time'

I am grateful for all the organisations around the world that work to liberate children from these horrific situations, but I've also seen that taking a child out of an army does not necessarily fill these fundamental needs. We have to do more for these children, to fill that void in their lives with love, an education, a community to give them a new purpose and allow them to find an opportunity to succeed. The light has never left these children. We just need to help them rediscover it.

This desire to empower young people to fill the unmet needs in their lives became the impetus behind the creation of my foundation, the Whitaker Peace & Development Initiative. We operate in parts of the world touched by conflict, from Uganda to Tijuana, from South Sudan to Los Angeles. We work with young women and men to help them develop the tools they need to become leaders and peacebuilders in their communities.

The challenges in many of the places where we work are truly daunting; there's a keen sense of struggle, pushing forward, making sure you keep your eyes open to the successes that are occurring in front of you. And there are successes. We started working in South Sudan in 2013, just a few months before civil war broke out and plunged the country into chaos and violence. When the fighting started, we had to suspend the programme. It was disappointing to be halting our progress, and it was absolutely heartbreaking to see how this tragedy was impacting our youth peacemakers.

Many of them were forced to leave their homes. Some lost family members. But in the midst of the violence and bloodshed, these young women and men – who came from different tribes and who, in many cases, found each other on opposite sides of the ethnic line that was dividing the country – reached out to one another and helped each other find safety.

They acted almost as an early-warning system, calling each other to say, 'don't go down that road, it's not safe for your tribe there'. These youth were taking what they had learned from the programme and using it to come together, to build peace, to save lives. It is these individual stories of love and strength – of boundless care for our fellow human beings – that give me hope, for South Sudan and for our world.

People and communities across the globe are confronting some massive challenges; from civil war, to abject poverty, to a climate that is changing before our eyes. When you look at these challenges from afar, it can be easy to feel overwhelmed by it all. That's why these stories of heroism and compassion matter so much. They are a reminder that there are lights inside all of us that persist despite the darkness. They make us believe that, one day, with our continued care, guidance and advocacy, these lights will come together to form a human flame of enduring peace – a fire bright enough to drive out any darkness. ○

'Individual stories of love and strength, of boundless care for our fellow human beings, give me hope for our world' ·

"There is a divine spark within every human being that gives all of us the capacity for extraordinary goodness"

Forest Whitaker

Acting local

Badr Jafar

Across the world, companies and entrepreneurs are increasingly looking to the power of social enterprise to help tackle the most pressing issues affecting their communities. Yet adopting a one-size-fits-all approach risks doing more harm than good. To make lasting progress, social enterpreneurs must tailor their responses to suit their local context, writes Badr Jafar

———————

Badr Jafar
CEO, Crescent Enterprises

THE AUTHOR

Badr Jafar, CEO of the UAE-based Crescent Enterprises, is a businessman and philanthropist. His charitable projects include the Pearl Initiative, a venture with the UN Office for Partnerships to promote corporate accountability in the Middle East, and he is a prominent advocate of social enterprise in the region

---

S tatistics, it is said, are the third kind of lie. This is something to keep in mind when measuring progress within societies. Take, for example, the figure that between 1981 and 2010, China lifted an estimated 680 million citizens out of poverty. While undoubtedly a great achievement, it must be balanced with the country's position as the world's largest emitter of greenhouse gases over the same period.

In the Middle East and North Africa, literacy rates have risen from 59 per cent to 78 per cent in just two decades. This is a welcome development, but can we really be satisfied when the level of youth unemployment in the region has simultaneously risen to nearly 30 per cent? In the US, the number of citizens with a college degree rose from 22 per cent in 1975 to 34 per cent in 2013. However, this has not prevented income inequality reaching its highest levels since the onset of the Great Depression, leading to the rise of another statistic – "the 1%" – as a popular refrain in American politics.

One conclusion to be drawn is that statistics can never portray the whole story. Another is that social progress is not a zero sum game, and while meaningful gains may be achieved in one area, there will always be work to do in another. An equally valid finding, in my view, is that social progress can only ever be fully understood in its own local context. Just as social and other challenges vary greatly between villages, cities and countries, so do the most appropriate solutions and their likely outcomes.

After all, the day-to-day challenges facing people in the UAE, for example, are as different to those facing their neighbours in Saudi Arabia as they are between the people of New York and London. Similarly, just because a particular solution works well in Malaysia does not necessarily mean it can be applied with the same success in neighbouring Indonesia. For the increasing number of businesses that have adopted a sense of purpose beyond simply generating profit, this is a critical point.

Across the world, and increasingly in the Middle East, you can find countless examples of companies seeking to apply the principles of social enterprise to tackle the most prominent issues of the day. As positive as this trend is, the temptation to apply one-size-fits-all business models must be avoided. Not only is a cookie cutter approach unlikely to succeed, it also has the potential to exacerbate social or economic problems.

For instance, social enterprises that provide finance to help people on low incomes purchase homes, have proven to be highly effective in well-regulated economies with properly functioning property markets. However when applied in countries with limited housing supply and different challenges, such as in Brazil's largest cities, these social enterprises have inadvertently led to land price inflation, poorer quality construction, and developments being built further from the city centre, separating some residents from basic public services.

Social enterprises must never lose sight of the local viability or applicability of their proposed solutions. The vast potential of social enterprise is most effectively unleashed when local solutions are applied to local situations. This does not mean social entrepreneurs cannot take inspiration from others, but when developing and refining their own business models, they must always consider local economic factors, social nuances, demographics and politics. They need to tailor their responses to the specific social, cultural, political and economic context in which they intend to create positive change.

An example of this is Glowork, a company founded in 2011, that has made a major contribution towards solving Saudi Arabia's female employment challenge. It matches Saudi women with jobs by seeking out roles in sectors previously inaccessible – or at least hard to access – for women.

With more than 30 percent of Saudi women unemployed, the need for creative, proactive solutions was self-evident. Yet taking off-the-shelf business models from elsewhere in the world was unlikely to work. Instead, Saudi-based Glowork developed its own simple, elegant and locally-relevant solution. Within four years, the company had built a network of 2,200 companies committed to recruiting more female candidates, and had helped more than 26,000 Saudi women find jobs.

By creating sustainable business models that are tailored to their surroundings, many social enterprises are repackaging capitalism and redefining what it means to be successful. No longer is capitalism merely the economic expression of survival of the fittest, but rather it can also be the sharpest and most effective tool for dealing with the myriad social challenges we face.

'With more than 32 per cent of Saudi women unemployed, the need for creative, proactive solutions is self-evident'

However, just as no single statistic can ever adequately measure progress within a society, no one model of social enterprise has all the answers to society's problems. The most effective approaches will always be those that take local factors into account. After all, if the power of Chinese commerce was able to pull millions out of poverty in a matter of decades, just think what the millions of social enterprises emerging around the world could achieve by thinking big and acting locally at the same time. ○

Africa's future

Reeta Roy

The magnitude of need in Africa is great; but with a new and growing population of young, smart and ethical leaders emerging on the continent, so is the potential. Reeta Roy explains how we can nurture and support this new generation of African business leaders and philanthropists – to make a brighter future for Africa

———

Reeta Roy
CEO, MasterCard Foundation

———

THE AUTHOR

Reeta Roy is president and CEO of the MasterCard Foundation, an independent body established in 2006 by MasterCard Worldwide. The foundation reaches more than 9 million people, principally in 29 countries in Africa, through its education, youth skills development and financial inclusion programmes

———

A few years ago, 15 young people from some of Senegal's poorest communities were telling me excitedly about their new ventures – entrepreneurial activities they hoped would set them on a more prosperous path and help others from similarly disadvantaged backgrounds. One young man dreamed of introducing more computers into primary schools; another had set up a network to help rural youth find their feet in the urban tumult of Dakar, the country's capital.

Just as I was leaving, I said: "What you are doing is wonderful. Your parents must be so proud." The response caught me off guard. Every single one replied, "My parents are against what I'm doing." They each faced family pressure to get a government job, or to use their English skills instead to become a tour guide.

Their stories are instructive in understanding some of the obstacles for ambitious African youth. The journey to work - whether formal or informal, entrepreneurship or traditional employment – is often a solitary one, with little practical support that might equip them with the skills, education and tools they need. Or, as illustrated in the case above, a favourable social environment to try something new.

Africa is home to the world's largest population of young people who, in about 25 years, will make up the largest workforce in the world. By some forecasts, 11 million young people are expected to enter Africa's labour market each year for the next decade. If countries on the continent can boost job growth and equip young people with the skills and practical experience necessary for work, then Africa has a significant opportunity to achieve rapid, inclusive and sustainable economic growth. Moreover millions will have the opportunity to lift themselves out of poverty. Early on at the MasterCard Foundation we chose to focus on Africa because we saw the magnitude of the gaps in access to secondary and higher education, and financial products and services.

Two billion people around the world lack access to financial services, according to the World Bank. In sub-Saharan Africa, just 34 per cent of adults have access to a bank account, making it difficult for people to put money aside for unplanned events – such as a food shortage or a crop failure – or education and other needs. And while progress has been made in access to education, still only around one-third of young people are enrolled in upper secondary school.

So we partnered with likeminded organisations to design programmes that create opportunities for people, especially for young people, to acquire the tools they need to transition out of poverty. In turn, these youth will help their families and communities to a brighter future, too.

The way we see it, our programmes are helping to educate and develop the next generation of African leaders, preparing those young people for the workforce and promoting inclusive finance and growth.

There is a rise – albeit modest at the moment – of an entrepreneurial cadre of young people who want to do business in a different way. At the foundation, we use the term 'transformative leadership'. It is about addressing inequity and making positive change to improve the lives of others. When I ask young people the question: "What will you do when you gain these skills or when you get a job?" The reply is almost always: "I will help somebody else like me."

Many of the students I meet through the MasterCard Scholars Program – an initiative to help more low-income African students into secondary school and on to university – are hungry for just such an opportunity. There are so many examples of young people from countries such as Ghana and Kenya who, immediately after graduation, return to their secondary school and inspire the children to follow them, encouraging them to work hard. Some have set up community projects in their villages to address HIV/AIDS, built shelters for orphans and young children, and better housing. They are role models of what is possible; they are examples of transformative leadership in action.

A new generation of educated and ethical entrepreneurs is emerging across the continent of Africa. They have the potential to drive change in their countries and communities, but they cannot do it all on their own. We need to nurture them, work with them, listen to their needs and desires, as they see them. If we do that, these leaders can be the key catalysts of transformation and the philanthropists of tomorrow. ○

'In sub-Saharan
Africa, still
only one-third of
young people are
enrolled in upper
secondary school'

'Around 11 million
young people are
expected to enter
Africa's labour
market each year for
the next decade'

The road ahead

Filippo Grandi

Without peace and a renewed commitment to addressing the needs
of Syrians displaced by conflict, millions of families will never be in a
position to return home. Filippo Grandi, head of the UN Refugee Agency,
describes how the global community might better support refugees and
the countries that host them

———————

Filippo Grandi
United Nations High Commissioner for Refugees

————

THE AUTHOR

Filippo Grandi is the 11th United Nations High Commissioner for Refugees, the head of the UN agency mandated with protecting the more than 65.3 million people who have been forced from their homes. He has been engaged in refugee and humanitarian work for more than 30 years, in Africa, Asia, the Middle East and Europe

——

M ohammed told me he did not want to spend his whole life on the run. His words, so simple, and yet so powerful, reflect the sentiment of millions of displaced people around the world. Many have given up hope that there will ever be a real solution and are willing to risk their lives not to endure another day in exile.

I met Mohammed during a visit to Jordan's largest refugee camp, Za'atari. When Mohammed, his wife and six children sought refuge in Jordan, he thought that they would only be there for six months. However, the months turned quickly into years and when I met the family, they had been in Za'atari for three years.

Often when we talk about displacement, people become statistics. They are reduced to a number of arrivals or a number of people in need. Yet the stories of these women, children and men, who have been forced to flee their homes by war and persecution and who lost everything, must be told. Telling their story is important to remind us that behind each statistic there is a person who needs our help.

Many will remember 2015 as the year of Europe's refugee and migration crisis, when more than 1 million people arrived by boat and made their way north under chaotic conditions. More than 86 per cent of the people arriving in Europe were from the world's top 10 refugee-producing countries. For the first time in many years, refugees were at the centre of the world's attention.

Yet this is not only a European phenomenon: we live in an increasingly dangerous world, and one in which more than 65 million people have been forcibly displaced. In the past five years, at least 15 conflicts have erupted or reignited. And with the world's most protracted crises continuing to fester, more people are stuck in exile, living half-lives. Third-generation refugees are born in countries such as Kenya, Pakistan and Sudan, and face uncertain futures.

'With the world's most
protracted crises
continuing to fester, more
people are stuck in exile,
living half-lives'

The years of exile have taken their toll on Mohammed and his family. The monthly financial assistance they receive barely covers their most basic needs. Coupled with frustration about the increasingly drawn-out nature of their displacement, he and his family are seriously contemplating returning to Syria, whether conditions are conducive or not.

The unfortunate reality is that inconsistent funding limits humanitarian response capacity and creates additional difficulties for both refugees and the communities who have been hosting them. The burden of care falls disproportionately on a small

number of countries based primarily on geography, because of their proximity to the conflict area. It is important to ensure that immediate humanitarian aid, while important and lifesaving, should not overshadow the support that is required to sustain the often long-term presence of displaced people in host communities.

Similarly, refugees' skills, education, talents and contributions to communities should not be underestimated. At the World Economic Forum in 2016, Jordan announced it would be willing to consider special economic zones for Syrian refugees, to provide a level of economic self-sufficiency and also lower the cost of hosting refugees. Such innovative solutions are truly a long-term vision towards supporting displaced people and their hosts, while recognising potential and focusing on local development.

I commend the countries and their citizens that have responded with compassion and humanity to the suffering of those fleeing conflict and desperation. They recognise that no parent chooses to put their children on unsafe boats or push them through barbed wire fences unless they really see no other way to get them to safety. However, the large numbers of refugees have overwhelmed neighbouring countries and the rest of the world needs to do more to support the services and facilities of host countries, to support economies that are reeling under the pressure of such a sudden and significant influx of people.

We have also appealed to the international community to do more by offering alternative pathways for the admission of Syrian refugees; for example, different forms of resettlement, more flexible mechanisms for family reunification, student visas and scholarship and medical visas. Initial results for Syrian refugees have been promising with more than 200,000 places promised, and we hope that this model can be replicated to help find solutions for other refugees who find themselves in a protracted situation.

We cannot allow desperate refugees to put their futures and the lives of their loved ones in the hands of smugglers. A more comprehensive global response is required to ensure that refugees have safe alternatives available to them to seek safety beyond the Middle East region. Without such options, restrictive measures impeding access only benefit the smuggling and trafficking networks that are profiting from the despair of tens of thousands of refugee families.

Unless we change the way we view displaced persons, and our approaches towards humanitarian assistance, from targeted short-term assistance to long-term development support, those affected by conflict will continue to suffer. The road ahead is challenging, but we can make progress if we – humanitarian and development organisations, governments, civil society, the private sector, the displaced people and their hosts – all work together, ensuring protection and improved living conditions for millions. o

Leading from the front

Joanne Liu

It has never been more dangerous to be a doctor on the frontlines, yet a moment's intervention can have benefits for generations to come. International president of Médecins Sans Frontières, Joanne Liu, explains why we must ensure the safety of aid workers if we are to secure a better future for all

————

Joanne Liu
International president, Médecins Sans Frontières

––––––––

THE CONTRIBUTOR

Dr Joanne Liu is international president of Médecins Sans Frontières (MSF), also known as Doctors Without Borders. A paediatrician by training, she first volunteered with MSF in 1996 before taking the helm in 2013. This essay was composed from an interview with Dr Liu

––––

H ow much difference can you really make in times of war or disaster? As doctors we can deliver emergency aid, treat the wounded, and try and stem the spread of disease.

Our impact on the frontlines goes beyond the single patient. We have a chance to help whole communities – present and future. When I was younger, a book that really moved me was Albert Camus' The Plague, about a disease that spreads rapidly through a North African town. When asked why he keeps going the protagonist replies, "I am still not used to seeing people die". None of us can get used to death, we must always do more.

Médecins Sans Frontières (MSF) mobilised doctors and nurses to help tackle the Ebola epidemic in March 2014. By June there were 60 different chains of transmission, but without the intervention of aid organisations there could easily have been hundreds. The death toll – high as it was – could have been in the millions. MSF had the know-how to act and it responded. However, early on it was apparent by its geographical spread that this Ebola epidemic was going to be different. When it became clear that the people present on the ground were losing the war against the virus but could win if more aid was mobilised, MSF used its voice to urge others to act.

Back in 1971, MSF grew as a result of the Biafran conflict, the civil war that engulfed Nigeria. In the 1970s and 1980s there were very few aid workers. That has changed dramatically and there are some 500,000 international relief workers employed by humanitarian actors today, as well as national responders. Over the decades the medical professionals who work with MSF and other organisations have been able to do so because of the cover afforded by the Geneva Conventions, a series of treaties signed in the aftermath of the Second World War to establish protections for the wounded and

'When it became clear that
those on the ground were losing
the war against Ebola but could
win if more aid was mobilised,
MSF used its voice to urge
others to act'

sick, and those caring for them. Doctors understand that they take risks operating in war zones, but the medical mission needs to be protected. If there is one word to sum up the difficulties we face as humanitarians today, it is access – access to populations, to healthcare, to innovation and to medicines.

On 3 October 2015, coalition forces bombed our trauma centre in the Afghan city of Kunduz. Forty-two people died, including 24 patients and 14 staff. An MSF-supported health structure was bombed or shelled every single week on average in Syria in 2015. Hospitals in the Central African Republic, Syria, Yemen and Ukraine have been bombed, raided, looted or burned to the ground. The UN verified 59 attacks against 34 hospitals worldwide in 2015. The impartial provision of healthcare is under attack, and hospitals are being dragged onto the battlefield. We need to uphold the laws of war, even as the nature of warfare changes.

Despite growing global humanitarian resources, the political will to respond to emergencies is often lacking. Globally, we have never witnessed so many people displaced and forced from their homes. Some 24 people escaped war, disaster or persecution each minute of every day in 2015, a four-fold increase on the previous decade.

Countries often look at problems through the wrong lens, weighing intervention against the political impact or the repercussions on national security interests. This has a negative impact on populations, on the readiness of a humanitarian response and also on its quality. What matters most is the medical and the humanitarian imperative – to do the most good we can, where we can. And we need help to make sure we can do that in relative safety – without the rights of people being flouted or International Humanitarian Law being violated. ○

"If there is one word to sum up the difficulties we face as humanitarians today, it is access"

———

City of opportunity

With 600,000 young Londoners considered to be living in poverty, social mobility was hot on the agenda for **Boris Johnson** when he took over as the city's mayor in 2008. Here, the founder of The Mayor's Fund for London explains why it was important to leave the UK capital in better health

———

Boris Johnson is UK Secretary of State for Foreign and Commonwealth Affairs. He was Mayor of London from 2008 to 2016, when he founded The Mayor's Fund for London, which has injected more than £13m ($19m) into charitable activities for underprivileged children in the UK capital. Here he talks about that legacy.

Your term as London's Mayor came to an end in May 2016. How did the capital evolve on your watch?

While I was Mayor, London's population swelled by 600,000 people; we expect the population to reach 10 million by 2030, and 11 million by 2050. This puts massive pressure on housing, transport and jobs.

I promised City Hall would deliver 100,000 affordable homes; we invested massively in public transport; and we've got record employment, hundreds of thousands of new apprenticeships and a London Living Wage benefiting 30,000 workers. We did a lot, but there's much more to do.

You created three charities during your tenure. What inspired this?

I stated in my manifesto [policy aims] that I wanted to found a charitable pot for London. So I created The

Mayor's Fund for London [Mayor's Fund], the Mayor's Music Fund and The Legacy List.

London is a city of incredible opportunity, a massively upward, mobile city. But not every Londoner benefits from the city's successes in the way that they should. There are too many kids growing up in poverty. Look at Queen Elizabeth Olympic Park, which has transformed a once derelict part of East London into a beautiful green space, a new destination, and an important cultural and education quarter.

The park is surrounded by four of the six poorest boroughs in the UK. You have the highest levels of child poverty, the highest levels of illiteracy and innumeracy. Here, in what is one of the most dynamic and successful economies in Europe, some of our kids are not getting fair chances. The Mayor's Fund is designed to break down the barriers that stunt aspiration, reduce educational attainment, stifle ability and ultimately block access.

Are you happy with the progress the charities have made so far?

I am very proud to say we have raised more than £20m since 2008. The Mayor's Fund has injected £13m into

helping to ensure that there is something out there for everybody. Be the Best You Can Be! is a wonderful legacy of London 2012 – the aspirational programme is using the values that underpin the Olympic Games to help coach young Londoners in the classroom. The beneficiaries I have spoken to are now aiming higher, and not only making plans to achieve their goal, but creating back-up plans in case 'Plan A' does not work out.

What is the mission of the Mayor's Fund?

We think that the best way to escape the threat of poverty and play a part in the future of London, is to get a job. The Mayor's Fund helps offer young people a chance to acquire the skills and seize the opportunities they need to do this. It can be as fundamental as providing a healthy breakfast so that kids are ready to focus for the day. For London to retain its status as one of the greatest cities on earth, it is vital that our young people have every opportunity to learn, and become the leading professionals of our next generation. Being numerate and literate is vitally important and The Mayor's Fund and its supporters are doing fantastic work to improve academic performance, raise confidence, change attitudes and share best practice in core skills across the city. In turn, this leads to great employment opportunities and the charity ensures that access channels are open through its job brokerage scheme, Young London Working, and apprenticeship and training programmes in the burgeoning creative and technology sectors.

How is the charity working towards social mobility?

London is one of the most successful cities in the world and as we emerge from the economic downturn The Mayor's Fund wants to ensure all young Londoners are able to share in our city's future success and prosperity. It's a matter of social justice. In a city of such opportunity, how can we tolerate kids leaving school unable to enter the economy because they don't have the key skills, or are simply unaware of the opportunities available?

What are some of the highlights of your time as patron of The Mayor's Fund?

The highlights are always meeting young people and visiting projects. I helped to launch London's Biggest Breakfast in 2014. I got beaten at a mental maths challenge by a 14 year-old in front of Rudy Giuliani [the former mayor of New York]. I celebrated the fund's fifth birthday

with its enigmatic youth board – a group of 14-24 year-old Londoners who help to inform the agenda for the charity – and I was extremely proud to celebrate the £20m raised with some of the beneficiaries.

What do you think is your legacy as Mayor and patron of The Mayor's Fund?

I have been privileged to be the Mayor of London, I thoroughly enjoyed every minute and I am proud of what we achieved, but there is still a lot of work to be done. We were working for social justice, putting the people who work hard at the heart of policy. It is of vital importance to continue investing in infrastructure and being positive about what Britain can achieve. We have the timezone, the languages, the creative sector and the technology sector to continue to be a dynamic economy that is ever-growing. By 2050, we will have the largest populous, and the most substantial economy in Europe. There has been unbelievable change in my lifetime. At the heart of this is the high value, service-based economy of London and the people who will play a huge part in its future. The Mayor's Fund is working tirelessly to transform the life chances of those who need it most.

You launched Penny for London for The Mayor's Fund in 2014 – tell us about this scheme.

Penny for London is a big, bold idea that will revolutionise the way we give to charity. The latest contactless technology is going to help transform the lives of thousands of young people across the capital. Enabling people travelling around the city to pool their pennies every day they travel or buy a coffee, could potentially add up to hundreds of thousands of pounds. And the best thing about it is just how simple it is: just sign up and tap in. The rapid rise in the use of contactless payments makes it a fuss-free way to support Penny for London and to help projects working tirelessly to help young people in our city.

What makes London so great?

Provided we continue to grow, and the transport infrastructure matches the growth in population and opportunity in the city, we will continue to be one of the best cities on earth. Thanks to the generosity of businesses and Londoners themselves, thousands of youngsters across the capital have benefited over the last eight years. I am immensely proud and grateful for the public spiritedness that is to be found in the city. o

Transforming communities

Fadi Ghandour

The Arab World is undergoing a transformation as rising unemployment and a lack of opportunity for young people place unsustainable strain on government resources. Fadi Ghandour urges the private sector to come forward and build a new model for development, to help shape a truly entrepreneurial society

———

Fadi Ghandour

Founder, Ruwwad for Development

––––––

THE AUTHOR

Fadi Ghandour is the executive
chairman of Wamda Capital and
the founder and vice chairman of
logistics conglomerate Aramex.
He is also, among many other
responsibilities, founder of
Ruwwad for Development, and a
member of the board at Endeavor
Global, a nonprofit dedicated to
high-impact entrepreneurship

––

I f this season of radical transformations has taught us anything, it is that governments alone – however well intentioned and willing – cannot be the sole agents of progress. In the Arab world, the prevailing model of development, centered on the state as the chief custodian and provider, has been fast eroding under the sheer weight of its unsustainability. By practically every measure, governments have been disappointing their citizenries. Entrenched poverty and unemployment and the confounding 'youth question' have become fixtures of life in every other Arab country.

The region is ready for a more inclusive developmental model. But what does this demand of us as socially-engaged citizens with a vested interest in progress? Let us begin with the fundamentals: the urgent need to create a new ecosystem that emphasises the intersection of interests and brings into one collaborative space the public and private sectors and civil society.

Each of these players is crucial to the struggle: they have expertise to leverage, resources to deploy, innovations to share. With an organising force their collective impact is very likely to be transformative; without it, their efforts, commendable though they might be, are sure to fall far short of their potential.

The challenge, of course, is to establish the working principles and identify the mechanisms, tools and know-how essential to the success of this ecosystem. This is where the private sector – with its ability to create jobs and wealth, its enterprising spirit and receptiveness to inventive solutions – is uniquely equipped to play a key role.

This would require the Arab private sector to come out of its self-imposed marginalisation and embrace the fact that its wellbeing is intertwined with that of society at large. It is no longer enough for

'Ruwwad now spans Jordan, Egypt,
Lebanon and Palestine, embedding
itself within underserved
neighbourhoods as an enabler and
facilitator of community action'

the sector to content itself with the act of charity. Its main mission now has to be that of helping shape a new entrepreneurial society that pushes us all forward.

Some of us have already started to move in that direction. The trigger for me was my growing frustration with the discourse on the youth of the region, dominant since the turn of this century, which framed 60 per cent of our population – those under 25 years of age – as a critical problem. The depiction is understandable. Our economies need to create 60 to 80 million jobs by 2020 just to maintain the current 25 per cent youth unemployment rate. Meanwhile, the serious mismatch between the skills learned in antiquated educational systems and the demands of a fast-changing job market grows worse, increasing pressure on already indefensibly high unemployment levels.

Yet precisely because of these unsettling realities, I became convinced that a different path is possible; that we, business entrepreneurs, are capable of building a new paradigm of social engagement. That we can help young citizens weave a new narrative, one in which they are the producers of solutions rather than the dreaded problem.

This passionate belief brought me together with a group of like-mined Jordanian entrepreneurs to imagine a dynamic space that provides young people with the opportunities and tools they need. It is a space that hosts different and alternative learning methods in preparation for the job market; a safe haven for inclusive dialogue and creativity; a character-building environment that nurtures activist leaders of the future through grassroots volunteerism and community mobilisation.

This is how, in 2005, Ruwwad for Development came to life as a community development initiative rooted in the unshakable conviction that solutions to problems within a community can only be engineered by the active participation of its members.

From its birthplace in Amman, Ruwwad now spans Jordan, Egypt, Lebanon and Palestine, embedding itself within severely underserved neighbourhoods as an enabler and facilitator of community action. From the outset it did not seek to impose answers, instead engaging in serious conversations with the communities' members and active youth, to inspire and develop grassroots initiatives that respond directly to their needs and priorities. Thus, the community becomes the author of its own solutions, with residents taking up the mantle of responsibility in serving their own neighbourhoods.

Ruwwad is fully sustained by the long-term, strategic engagement of private sector entrepreneurs, whose support extends beyond the organisation's annual endowment to putting their commitment, experience and reach to use in advancing Ruwwad's goals, foremost among them the promotion of activism and human agency.

Take Ruwwad's scholarship fund: students earn the financial support to acquire formal degrees in exchange for devoting four hours a week to volunteering and community organising; today these students donate a total of 84,600 hours annually. The components of this programme also encompass character-building workshops, mentorships by experts, and job placements through partnerships. This is how, every year, more than 450 young Ruwwad scholars across the four countries enrol and actively help their local communities to break out of marginalisation.

Ruwwad also creates a safe space for the youth to discuss ideas freely, and to be exposed to new experiences that shift traditional boundaries. Weekly meetings dubbed *Dardashat* (Arabic for 'dialogues'), allow boys and girls to interact and address pressing issues in their communities.

In one such interactive workshop, Ruwwad citizens discussed the meaning of literacy, probing the question of how to inspire a culture of reading in their community. Mothers, teachers, librarians and students created the Six Minutes Campaign, encouraging six minutes of reading for leisure every day. The idea inspired 5,000 participants to commit to reading within their homes, schools and neighbourhood libraries.

In Tripoli, Lebanon, those same discussion groups have brought together students from two different sects of Islam, the Sunnis and the Allawis. Through critical conversations, those students have been enabled to discover and discuss their similarities and their shared experiences, needs and aspirations – not their differences – creating common ground for collaboration.

The proactive mindset Ruwwad cultivates has other effects: it inspires its graduates to become inventive entrepreneurs. For example Ala'a Salal, a graduate of Ruwwad and a very ambitious young man, created Jamalon, the world's largest online Arabic and English bookstore.

When this entrepreneurial environment began to take shape in the community, we launched, in 2012, the Ruwwad Micro-Venture Fund, the first microequity fund supporting marginalised communities in Jordan. Through a joint funding initiative with the United Nations Development Programme, the fund provided microentrepreneurs with up to $9,000 in equity, with the aim of creating three jobs per business. Within two years, the programme succeeded in launching more than 140 microbusinesses in local communities creating 420 jobs, while 50 per cent of those businesses were cash flow positive from the first year of operation.

Ruwwad's scale so far is modest. However envisage the reach and impact of such private sector efforts if they were to become an integral part of a new development model – one through which we in the Arab world might reimagine the future to be infinitely more promising. ○

World in action

Princess Astrid of Belgium

Roll Back Malaria has averted more than 6 million malaria-related deaths since 2000. Princess Astrid of Belgium, a former special representative for the charity, describes her passion for the battle against the disease and explains why the public-private partnership is an example of the good we can do together

---

Princess Astrid of Belgium
Former special representative, Roll Back Malaria

————

THE AUTHOR

Princess Astrid of Belgium
served as special representative
of the Roll Back Malaria
Partnership from 2007 to 2015, an
organisation which helps
save millions of lives. She was
also chair of the Belgian Red
Cross, and sits on the Honorary
Board of the International
Paralympic Committee

——

T he idea that certain fragments of the world's population are being left behind by global development efforts has been a driving force in my engagement with charitable organisations, encouraging me to leverage my public platform to offer a voice to the voiceless, and ensure their inclusion in processes beyond their reach.

This commitment to a better, more just and more prosperous world, where all are granted opportunity to thrive, has led me to serve as the chairwoman of the Belgian Red Cross from 1994 to 2007 and a member of the honorary board of the International Paralympic Committee since 2009. It also made it easy to answer the request of the Roll Back Malaria (RBM) Partnership – a global coordinating mechanism attached to the United Nations – when I was asked to join as their special representative in 2007 to help advance efforts against malaria under the UN's Millennium Development Goals (MDGs).

Over the next eight years, I travelled to some of the most remote areas of the world with RBM, visiting government leaders and policymakers, researchers and community health workers. From Tanzania and Zambia, to Kuwait, the UAE and Saudi Arabia, to Cambodia, Indonesia, the US and Japan, among others, I visited government buildings and humble health facilities to encourage greater resources and political commitment for malaria control and elimination; to stop the spread of a preventable and treatable disease transmitted by the bite of a tiny infected mosquito. Through the RBM Partnership, I have witnessed unimaginable sacrifices made by parents. I have sat with grieving mothers, watched fathers dig graves to hold the lifeless body of their young child, and I have sat in classrooms devoid of healthy students able to learn. On my first trip with RBM, I found myself in a rural Tanzanian hospital, huddled with mothers keeping watch over an alarming number of ailing children fighting for their lives. We'd walked very different paths, those women and I, but in that moment, tears flowed freely down our faces all the same. While visiting Indonesia, I was equally moved when I met a young man in a district hospital suffering from cerebral malaria. In and out of consciousness, the boy writhed in pain caused by an untreated malaria parasite that had spread to his brain. As we sat together quietly, I clutched his hand tight while his mother and I shared a silent glance that spoke volumes.

As a mother of five, these experiences have resonated with me on a deeply emotional level. The pain I have seen never leaves me, but it is made less by the profound hope that I have felt radiate throughout communities thanks to incredible, cost-effective tools, such as insecticide-treated nets, rapid diagnostic tests and artemisinin-based combination therapies, all of which have revolutionised the way we prevent, diagnose and treat malaria. These advancements – and the scale-up of their delivery – are largely the result of increased commitment and coordination under the RBM Partnership. As international investments in malaria control and elimination have risen from less than $100m in 1998 to $2.7bn annually in 2013, RBM has averted more than 6 million malaria-related deaths since 2000 – 97 per cent of which would have been children aged under five. Because of such investments, more than 100 countries are now free from malaria and the global MDG target for malaria has been achieved and in some cases even surpassed.

RBM's work in this regard is nothing short of remarkable. Today, with the MDGs just behind us and the new 2030 targets outlined in the Sustainable Development Goals, global poverty continues to decline, more children than ever are attending primary school, child deaths have dropped dramatically and targeted investments in health have saved millions. Our collective efforts are working; there's no question about it. This unprecedented progress would not have been possible without the support of the international aid community and political and business leaders. The Gulf Cooperation Council region, in particular, has been a proven ally in the fight against malaria, with the state of Kuwait, the Kuwait Fund for Arab Economic Development, the UAE, the Islamic Development Bank and Saudi Arabia each supporting global malaria efforts through commitments to bodies such as the World Health Organisation (WHO), the RBM Partnership and the Global Fund to Fight AIDS, TB and Malaria. But more is needed. In 2015 alone, WHO projections estimated 472,000 malaria-related deaths around the world, with more than 200 million cases burdening health systems and reducing economic productivity in some of the world's weakest communities. More than half the malaria burden is felt in countries of the Organisation of Islamic Cooperation.

'Aided by international investment, RBM has averted more than 6 million malaria deaths since 2000'

If we are to reach the 2030 target for malaria elimination, in excess
of $100bn will be needed. It's a high price tag, but the benefits we
stand to receive if we eliminate malaria will far surpass the initial
costs. We have already seen that for every $1 we invest in malaria
efforts in Africa, there is an increase in per capita GDP of $6.75.
If we can meet the financial demands and eliminate malaria by
2030, experts estimate that nearly 3 billion malaria cases will be
averted and over 10 million lives saved. In addition, our efforts
could generate upwards of $4 trillion of additional economic output
between 2016 and 2030, and would help strengthen entire systems
so limited human and financial resources can be shifted to more

"The pain I have seen never leaves me, but it is made less by the profound hope I have felt radiate from communities thanks to cost-effective tools"

———

pressing health needs. For me, it has always been a no-brainer, and this growing evidence makes it even clearer. By investing in malaria, we save lives and drive progress against the broader development agenda – we keep children in school and parents at work, while markets expand and societies become more stable.

As the MDGs have drawn to a close, along with my mandate with the RBM Partnership, which ended in 2015, it is clear that continued progress will require bold commitment and partnership from us all, regardless of position, within and between sectors. The development landscape is shifting, and as a result, so is foreign aid. Direct foreign assistance or investment is no longer sufficient on its own. Today, our world is more interconnected than ever before – with a record number of migrant communities, 62 million young girls unable to access education and diseases that transcend borders and permeate communities. These are not isolated issues particular to certain areas of the world; they are global issues and they threaten each of us, regardless of nationality, faith community or socioeconomic

class. The 2030 Agenda for Sustainable Development, which was adopted by world leaders in September 2015 during the UN General Assembly and includes 17 interconnected goals, accounts for this – but now our giving practices must adapt to respond to and deliver on this framework. If we are to deliver on the promises our leaders have made to the people of the world, we must all be global citizens and take up our responsibilities regardless of position. Whether a concerned individual, a researcher or a corporate executive, we all have a role to play as we work to create a healthier, more prosperous world.

Whether it's giving of time or money, using skills to help governments better capture and utilise data, or leveraging corporate positioning to protect employees, we all play an important part in this great story, and we can't stand by silently. As we set out toward 2030, with our sight on ambitious and comprehensive goals that will deliver a prosperous, more just and equitable world for its 7 billion inhabitants, let us do so together, with great vigour and focus. o

'If we are to deliver on the
promises our leaders have made
to the people of the world, we
must all be global citizens and
take up our responsibilities'

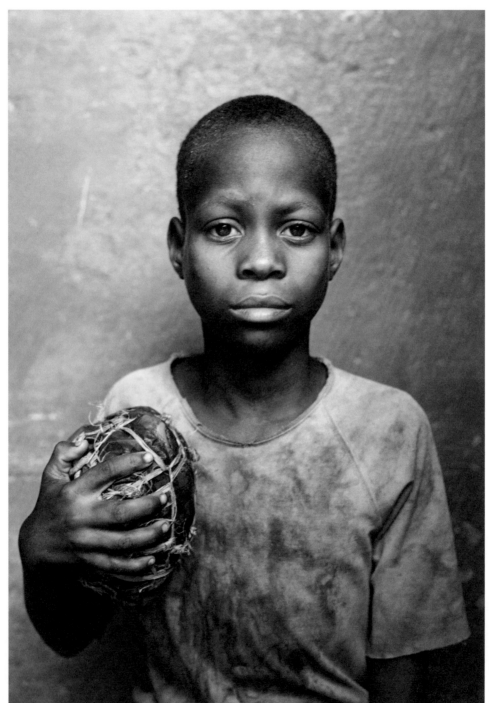

Life goals

Frédéric Oumar Kanouté

Faith is about the hands as well as the heart. Former footballer and humanitarian Frédéric Oumar Kanouté takes us on his personal journey from the football pitches of Europe to the villages outside the Malian capital Bamako, and a unique community project helping orphans to rebuild their lives

———

Frédéric Oumar Kanouté

Founder, Kanouté Foundation

———

THE AUTHOR

Frédéric Oumar Kanouté is a former footballer that played at the top level in France, England, Spain and China. He now dedicates his efforts to his eponymous foundation, which among other projects has built a community for orphans in Mali and seeks to relieve the suffering of the most vulnerable children

—

W hen I was in my early 20s and playing professional football in England, I began to practise my religion properly and also took a few trips to my father's homeland of Mali. I thought that my purpose in life was not just to enjoy all the luck I had, but to share it with people who need it most, and in Mali, I saw that there were huge problems with poverty. Life expectancy was low and many children had been orphaned. I resolved to try and build a village where we could cater to all the needs of the kids – from the age of five years – and take care of their education, health and training, as they grew older.

I wanted to build a village where the children could feel part of a real family with sisters, brothers and 'foster mothers' that live with them. Today at Sakina Children's Village we have a school, medical centre and teaching programmes, as well as a number of other facilities. Most importantly, education and skills training is at the core of what we do: because if you take care of the kids but don't give them any training, they will become too old to stay, but unable to leave because they can't do anything else. The children need to be self-sufficient, so that they can live their own lives, fly with their own wings, and perhaps one day even help the village in turn.

The complex is 30km away from the Malian capital Bamako, but we take kids from all over the country. We have around 65 children but the total capacity is up to 150 and there is a lot of demand for places. We go through applications very carefully and it's difficult but we have to decide which children to prioritise. We investigate the family situation of every child, analysing what kind of family is left to take care of them. Yes they are orphans, but do they still have aunts or uncles that can support them throughout their life?

We have to find those who are the most vulnerable. It is sad to say but many of the children arrive with some issues and many are traumatised by their previous lives. It takes time for us to reassure them, to give them back their confidence, and to teach them how to live a structured lifestyle with school, family and a routine. Eventually, they learn to smile again.

While I launched the children's village with my own funds, we really wanted to involve others and move forward with partners. I tried to make the most of my media profile to organise charity events with organisations such as the children's agency UNICEF, and big charity games with famous football stars from around the world.

'My purpose in life was not just to enjoy all the luck I had, but to share it with people who need it most'

Most of the players we called were happy to come and help, and these funds – along with personal donations through the foundation – have helped to support the project. Other organisations have helped in different ways; Qatar Charity, for example, has built a mosque at the entrance of the children's village, for the use of the local community.

In addition, the school, the health centre, the training centre and other facilities are open to the local community. They pay a small fee that goes towards the funding of the village, and we are also running livestock and agriculture projects that will help us in the future so that we do not have to rely on external funds. We think the children's village can be self-sufficient within two or three years.

I spent a lot of time during my career on this project. During my holidays I would always go to Mali, and daily, after training, I would be in contact with the foundation managers. While I was on duty with the national team, I would always make time to go and visit the village. It was quite a rare thing for a footballer to be doing, although I'm not saying that footballers don't help. They do, and when they do they're generous.

However, the children's village was part of my own fulfilment and so I was more involved personally, from a young age. I wanted to make sure that nobody deceived me or took advantage. We have been very careful to do everything in a very transparent way because this kind of work is very sensitive – you have to make sure that all the funds raised to go to a specific project actually do go directly to that purpose. Even with the best of intentions, mistakes can still be made.

In my personal experience, my faith has been the engine. Faith, if you practise it correctly, pushes you to commit good acts. Sometimes we say faith is only in the heart, but I don't think that's true. It is in the hands as well. In the Quran we always put the faith in partnership with the actions: "Those who have faith and do good." It rarely says: "Those who have faith alone."

I also believe that it is important to talk publicly about giving. While it is encouraged to give without people knowing, players can also use their profile to influence others and perhaps inspire them to emulate that player. It's all about the intention. If you talk about your philanthropic work out of pride then that's not positive, but if you talk about it because you want people that like you to emulate what you are doing, then that's good.

One day my little girl had to make a presentation on charity work at her school. She asked me about Sakina and based her presentation on that. I was so happy because I saw that it could influence her to go on and do this kind of work in the future. I wouldn't mind if, one day, people didn't remember me as a footballer, or remember my career. I believe I'm going to my creator and that He won't ask me how many goals I've scored, but instead will hold me accountable for how I behaved on this Earth, and how I helped others. ○

"Sometimes we say faith is only in the heart, but I don't think that's true. It is in the hands as well"

Frédéric Oumar Kanouté

Personal growth

Özlem Denizmen

Armed with the right information, individuals can make the right choices about their personal finances with life-changing effects. Turkish TV host Özlem Denizmen shows how financial inclusion can empower a new generation of Middle Eastern women and teach them to dream

———

Özlem Denizmen
Founder, Para Durumu

––––––––––

THE AUTHOR

Özlem Denizmen has led the Turkish financial empowerment movement since 2010. She is founder of the Financial Literacy and Inclusion Association of Turkey, and founded Para Durumu that aims to raise financial inclusion in Turkey and the wider Middle East through TV, radio, print media and workshops

––––

Z uhal Sonmez, 35, was used to life in debt. Barely able to keep up with her credit card repayments, there was little chance to put away money for the family's future in Mersin, a city in southern Turkey. But some simple advice on paying off debts transformed Zuhal's life. "I became successful in managing my money, like a queen ruling a country," she says now. Able to save and put aside TRY10-20 ($3-$6) a week for her son, the outlook is very different for Zuhal and the Sonmez family; her dream is to buy a new house.

This tale shows how something seemingly so small can make a big difference. Armed with the right information, individuals – and particularly women – can make the right choices about their personal finances with life-changing effects. That is the power of financial literacy.

Sadly, too many still miss out. Vulnerable and needy groups are trapped by poor financial literacy – lacking the skills and knowledge to make informed choices – or locked out of essential financial services. Financial empowerment has two sides: one is inclusion, which is about access and being in the system; the other is literacy, or knowing how to use it.

Globally, according to 2014 data, there are some 2 billion people that are not included in the financial system and only 14 per cent of the adult population in the Middle East has a bank account. Women are more likely to be unbanked, with studies showing just 58 per cent of women worldwide are banked, compared to 65 per cent of men. In short, there is a vast gender gap.

Women don't have control over wealth. They often don't have direct access to employment, which comes with a salary and thus immediate opening of a bank account, and in many countries there is less emphasis on education for women and girls, which harms their chances to be in the workforce. As poverty increases, financial inclusion and literacy fall.

Culture and tradition are often barriers. If your mother doesn't have a bank account or doesn't say anything about budgeting, you don't think girls should know about that sort of thing. Adult women impose limits on themselves, bending to the trope that they don't understand something so complicated as money, saying it is a father or brother's affair.

Yet financial inclusion of women is vital: it is good for individuals, and good for society. When women make money or take charge of household budgets, the funds flow back into the family. They go into nutrition, into education and into health, all of which are crucial development issues. According to World Bank and UN studies, women reinvest around 90 per cent of income into the family – that's more than twice as much as men.

Savings rates also increase. For women especially, one of the most important things is to secure their and their children's futures, not least because – as they live longer – the majority of women will be alone at some point in their lives.

Normally there is this wall of perception that managing money is hard; that it's maths. But once that wall is broken it benefits the family, because most of the education about money happens at home – from seeing what your parents do – and that trickles down to the next generation. So the benefits are obvious and immediate.

Yet if you want to do good, you have to hold hands: boosting financial inclusion cannot be achieved by the private sector, government or civil society on its own. We need public-private partnerships and we need innovative ways of increasing access to financial education, through traditional means and also utilising the revolution in online and experiential learning.

Media has a very strong role to play here. Para Durumu's TV show on everyday finances aimed at women reaches some four million people weekly in Turkey, where only 40 per cent of women are banked. Other media, whether through online media groups or through Whatsapp and Facebook groups, can take advantage of the fact women learn better together. We need to find ways to give women access to capital, give women networks, and give women equal access to opportunity.

We also need role models and to have those role models showcased. Above all, women need to be inspired and to dream. We run free financial literacy seminars and in all of these sessions I see that women don't dream. It is not just society's role to empower women; women have to break free from the barriers that they themselves construct. Finance is a means to an end: security, a holiday, a car, or a child's education. We need to get women dreaming and confident so they can radiate this confidence to the rest of the world. Societal and cultural norms take decades to shift. Yet already I see the new generation is better at talking about money in part because of the 2008 global financial crisis, the rise of the sharing economy and the Middle East's imperative to create millions of entrepreneurs in the next 15 years, all of which are spurs to understand better how to find and manage money.

In an ideal world, we would see an increase in the number of women at the table talking about money. And when conversations about finance start – whether in the home, in the workplace, or even on the bus – women would be part of those discussions. In the future I see women as interested in money as men. Some two decades from now, I hope the gender gap will be closed in terms of financial inclusion and we will see women with just as much opportunity to invest as men.

When women have access to services and the know-how to secure their financial future, they gain in confidence and feel empowered. And when a woman is happy and confident, the whole family is happier and more confident – just ask Zuhal. ○

"It is not just society's
role to empower women; women
have to break free from the
barriers that they themselves
construct"

The power of sharing

Social media has the power to move the digital world in which we live. Film star **Yao Chen**, dubbed the 'Queen of Weibo' in China, describes how she uses her influence to engage and inform millions of Chinese people of the plight of refugees worldwide

Actress Yao Chen is a household name in China. With more than 79 million followers on Weibo, the Chinese equivalent of Twitter, her social media outreach surpasses that of Barack Obama, Kim Kardashian and Justin Beiber. Since 2010 she has also campaigned tirelessly for UNHCR, the UN refugee agency, which in 2013 appointed her as its first ever goodwill ambassador to China. She uses her popularity to advocate fiercely for refugees around the world, from Asia to Africa and the Middle East.

How did your journey with UNHCR begin?

The UN refugee agency has had offices in China since the 1980s, yet most Chinese people have little idea what the agency does, or even what a refugee really is. I was the same, until by chance in 2009 I got to know some people from UNHCR, and they asked me if I would be their honourary patron in China. This was something new for the both of us: for the refugee agency to use a public figure to reach out to ordinary people in China, and for me to learn about refugees and their plight. It was an invitation I accepted with passion, and one that would change my life.

What have you learned about refugees since then?

I am still learning and my understanding grows with every visit to the field. One memory stands out, when I was in Ethiopia and we visited a family in their home. Their little boy was beautiful and during the conversation he leaned against me so sweetly that I could feel his warmth. When we made to leave he shifted his weight and I realised for the first time that his legs were rotten, and that he would not live much longer. I was heartbroken and I was aware suddenly of the depth of pain and struggle endured by some refugees; I understood that their suffering was terrible and that their strength to endure remarkable.

It is at times like that that as a visitor, you feel as though you cannot really help such people. I have seen the tears of many children, flies gathering on wounded feet, a camp built with nothing but thorns and plastic bags. You feel useless; how can you really make a difference when so many people are living in such misery?

However, I realised that this is when I am needed, that I can give refugees a voice. I can share their stories and make sure the world doesn't leave them behind.

Over time I have come to understand that a 'refugee' is not just a concept. It is a human being, an individual with

needs that we must try to meet. I can carry that message and when in 2013 the UNHCR asked me to become the first goodwill ambassador to China, I humbly agreed.

How valuable a tool has social media been, in telling these stories?

People relate more easily to personal experiences, and Weibo is a way in which I can communicate my personal feelings and thoughts to a wide audience. It has been really important in terms of telling the stories of refugee communities, and since 2010 I have shared experiences in Hong Kong, the Philippines, Thailand, Ethiopia and Syria.

The feedback has been enormous and I have had criticism as well as support. Some question why I am highlighting the poor of other countries when there are impoverished Chinese at home. Others say that I am doing this work as a way of showing off. This saddens me. However, I believe my role is to build understanding and battle against ignorance, and if that begins with changing the minds of those who do not care about refugees or even know what they are, then that is where I will begin.

Are people getting the message?

I believe so. One sign is that since 2010, UNHCR funding from China has grown tenfold, an amazing increase. Another sign is that now when I share information about refugees, if people post unfriendly messages then other Weibo users will come to my aid, explaining what refugees are and why they need help and support. That is very moving, to realise that others are learning and will step forward with passion to share and reinforce the same message.

Can ordinary people, everyday Chinese, also make a positive difference using social media?

You may think: how can I really make a difference when so many people are living in such misery? But absolutely you can. Even if you don't have as many followers as a public figure might, every time you share a piece of news you help more people – whether friends, colleagues or family – to understand and to know something. The power of sharing is enormous, and the more people are educated about important issues, the more likely they are to try and do something about them. UNHCR statistics in China show that more and more funding comes from individuals, so don't underestimate the difference you can make: you really can change the world. ○

On being human

Farahnaz Karim

There is no single path on the journey to doing good. It is, however, more important than ever to measure the ongoing impact of doing good, and to have the end-user at the heart of this process, writes Farahnaz Karim, founder of nonprofit social enterprise Insaan Group

———

Farahnaz Karim
Founder, Insaan Group

———

THE AUTHOR

Farahnaz Karim is a political scientist, development entrepreneur and academic, as well as a mother passionate about legacy. A former country director for French NGO ACTED in Afghanistan, and UN field officer, she is also the founder of social enterprise Insaan Group

—

I n graduate school we were asked to write our own obituary – an exercise I highly recommend. It seemed a little morbid at the time, but mine contained quite a bit on 'how to do, and be, good'. And it still would. But, how do you do it? Humankind has struggled to tackle this question for thousands of years.

Most belief systems try to guide us towards living a good and moral existence, despite unintended consequences. However, what it means to be moral, or to 'do the right thing' in today's parlance, takes a slightly different dimension in a world where both wealth and inequality have reached unprecedented levels. Never in human history have we come close to a scenario where, proportionately, the richest 300 people on earth have amassed the same amount of wealth as the next 3 billion people sharing the planet.

This shocking level of inequality, however morally disturbing and generally unsustainable, is precisely what struck me on a visit to Calcutta, India, as a child with my family in 1983: how crowded, how polluted and how unfair it was that children my age, who even looked like me, were sleeping on the streets.

That unsettling memory has stayed with me ever since. And so have many more from my time in the field. Memories of women who had been raped in Bosnia during the war, and of homes deliberately targeted because of the religion or ethnicity of a particular group. Women made invisible by the Taliban in Afghanistan; the fear of voting for a preferred candidate. The sight of destitute orphans in that country's capital, Kabul, and the abject poverty among Afghans displaced in their own country. And also the deplorable working conditions of craft workers in the slums of Nairobi.

But in every crisis zone and stricken country I have worked, I have always been amazed at the astonishing resilience of the human

race, and its ability to seek and stay hopeful for better times. This is how Insaan, which means 'human', emerged. It was born from the reality that we are all connected, all in search of better – of a life fulfilled. A not-for-profit social enterprise, Insaan brings together a group of committed international experts with some generous and inspirational funders. In that paradigm, those who are both fortunate and motivated – philanthropists – play a key role in reducing inequality, making many lives better, and in so doing derive a deep sense of fulfillment.

But if 'how to be good' takes work, how to actually do good is even more challenging.

In the field, one quickly learns that the machinery of aid and philanthropy often operates on autopilot, like an industrial-era factory scene from one of Charlie Chaplin's silent movies. There is considerable attention focused on all of the inputs – money, effort, and personal egos – but much less care taken about what comes out of that system.

The idea of measuring not just the money we disbursed, or the schools we built, but of going much further – actually analysing the educational outcomes, and staying engaged longer-term to measure how they will transform the lives of children – is still fairly new, but it is something Insaan has embraced, and sits at the heart of our approach.

Insaan works with philanthropists who want their giving to be more impactful. We call it high impact philanthropy. We do this by investing in innovative social enterprises that create opportunities for the poor through education and entrepreneurship.

Despite the recent development of impact metrics within philanthropy, the original conundrum has not yet been fully resolved. In a business, the market offers the feedback loop to establish that the product or service provided is relevant. In philanthropy and aid, the poor cannot shop around for the best nonprofit or aid agency, nor can they call to complain that the school that has been built has no trained teacher, or that the well has a broken hand pump.

Because of this basic missing piece, the equivalent of the market mechanism, we believe the end-user needs to be consulted to determine actual value, to define the metrics that have changed his or her life, and ultimately to define what it means to be successful when it comes to philanthropy and doing good. Not the metrics concocted in a boardroom, but the real world metrics of change that the end-user will use to measure how their lives have improved or been impacted.

Another unintended consequence of this conceptual peculiarity is that the response of many organisations now active in this space is often over-simplified: they mistakenly believe that for greater results or impact, one should focus on for-profit entities only. Again, the reality on the ground is slightly more complex. While backing

Insaan Group social investments include Gyan Shala, a low cost, high quality school model operating in Gujarat, Bihar, Uttar Pradesh, and West Bengal, transforming the lives of more than 45,000 slum children

for-profits can make sense to create large-scale employment, or support an innovation, the market is not always right, nor is the market solution always the best choice for the poorest in society.

Consider elementary education. Shouldn't high quality elementary school be a universal right for everyone, regardless of the capacity to pay?

Insaan is a humble response to these two systemic weaknesses: the need to put the end-user at the centre of any measurement, and the still fairly unusual thesis that both great nonprofits and innovative for-profit ventures can and should be supported by the philanthropic world.

We have learned much on our journey. We know that to reduce inequality and build inclusive economies, one has to start with investing in high-quality education early on. Sometimes that is achieved by backing an impactful, scalable nonprofit, and sometimes disruption is best introduced by for-profit models.

We have learned that investing in for-profit social enterprises may in some cases be more effective in creating large-scale, more sustainable employment, or backing the innovation of a particular product or service that the poor actually need. Hence, we are open to all sectors that are relevant to end-users, and to the country or countries of interest. Insaan takes an equity stake and financial returns are reinvested – thereby further multiplying the impact of any donation.

We know that regardless of the legal nature of the entity, both financial and social metrics matter; the same level of financial accountability and cost effectiveness applies. What is more, the same rigour in consulting end-users, the people we are servicing at every stage, should also apply in measuring that we are indeed changing lives for the better – and hopefully for the many.

We have learned that doing good seriously is similar to building an investment portfolio: you need diversification. At any one time the portfolio may include support for relief efforts, philanthropic investments in organisations like Insaan, or financial investments that also aim to address or redress societal ills. Investments across the whole range are not mutually exclusive.

On the entrepreneurial journey towards being good, and doing one's part to heal the world, there is no single path; no two identical journeys or ideal answers. There are only multiple narratives or facets of the human experience. The departure point, however, is often a sense of awareness about how we are all connected, about what it simply means to be human. ○

Insaan Group has joined other early investors to help develop a technology company called Soko, which connects small-scale artisans in Kenya to global consumers of ethical fashion, and in doing so provides a living to a growing number of families and dependents

Generations for good

Inheriting the principle of giving back is just as important as acquiring the family wealth. **Peggy Dulany** explains how philanthropy can be a tool to pass values down the generations, such as integrity and how to be a good global citizen

———

Born Peggy Dulany Rockefeller – one of the fourth-generation 'cousins' to hold the famous name – Peggy Dulany knows a thing or two about high-profile philanthropic dynasties. Putting her knowledge and networks to use, in 1986 she founded the US-based nonprofit Synergos Institute, dedicated to facilitiating relationships between people and institutions committed to overcoming poverty around the world. One of Synergos' key tenets is the importance of peer learning: whether among civil society leaders from more than 50 countries, or within the organisation's network of 300 social entrepreneurs in the Middle East and North Africa. Here, she talks about having a famous name, and how philanthropy is a valuable tool for families to pass on a culture of giving.

What is the ethos of the Global Philanthropists Circle (GPC), one of Synergos' initiatives?

The GPC is an invitation-only network of leading philanthropic families from all over the world committed to using their time, influence and resources to fight global poverty and social injustice. We have more than 100 families – some 250 individual philanthropists – from 31 different countries in the Circle.

Circle members are giving internationally with a focus on poverty alleviation. We welcome members who are interested in collaboration and in exchanging ideas with other philanthropists on how to make their philanthropy more impactful. All of our members give more than $1m annually, some a great deal more, or are involved with strategic interventions that are innovative. It is a peer-learning network – members learn from each other. We also help them connect to a personal sense of purpose with their philanthropy, and be more effective at collaboration, both with groups they wish to help and other actors. Our aim is to have members from all the regions where Synergos works. For example, we have four members from the Middle East and North Africa (MENA) region, of which two are from the Gulf.

How can philanthropy help pass on family values?

When the GPC started, one of the issues that surprised us was the focus on intergenerational transfer of values, as well as wealth. Often the grandparents, or parents, were concerned about whether they were bringing up their children to be responsible adults who could succeed them not only in business, but also in philanthropy.

The next generation, too, had many questions about how they could carry on the family legacy. They had questions such as, 'how can I live up to the patriarch in the family?' or, 'am I good enough?' We also saw the younger generation rebelling and wanting to go off on their own and do something quite separate.

Values are something we hold at the mega level. Believing in giving back is a value; believing in living with integrity is a value. My personal hope is that – using philanthropy as a tool – families can encourage the next generation to explore and experience different things, but to have those experiences with a view towards how they can develop and become good global citizens.

How has your own family been involved in the GPC?

I cofounded the GPC in 2001 with my father, David Rockefeller. He was 85-years-old at the time. He was nominally retired from his banking career and had reached a stage of life that I would call generativity – of wanting to mentor and support others, and foremost among those to mentor and support his children.

I felt humbled by the opportunity to found GPC with him and he was very keen to help push me forward. We bring different things to the table; he was perfectly willing to use his credibility, and the visibility of the Rockefeller name for example, to attract philanthropists to the Circle.

GPC membership is always by family. We aim for a mix of members: those who are just starting out and want to learn from a big global group, and those who are already at a more strategic point in their philanthropy. We aim to establish a safe space where people can listen openly to each other, exchange ideas and swap lessons.

Do you see appetite for that intergenerational transfer of values in the Middle East?

Over the past decade, philanthropy, and strategic philanthropy, in MENA has grown exponentially. There are a few notable exceptions, but generally families who have adopted this philosophy are just now starting to think about how to pass on these important values to their children.

The parents are starting to ask questions about how growing up with wealth – which they might not have done – will change attitudes, and how they should deal with that dilemma. I think in the region, so far, the first generation is thinking more about this issue than the next generation.

How did the weight of family expectation affect your own philanthropic journey?

In my own family there was a strong feeling that if you make a lot of money you have a responsibility to give back. By the fourth generation, I think philanthropy is practically in the genes. This doesn't just mean giving alms to the poor, but is an impetus to find the most strategic interventions you can that will help build the environment in which people can create jobs, promote wellbeing and good health, for example.

Yet starting out with such a famous name is a weighty thing. As a young woman I went to Brazil to do a research project and lived in a squatter's settlement in Rio de Janeiro. A journalist discovered I was there. I had been sheltered from the press my entire life and I was ill-equipped to manage the situation – so I fled. It was not a very constructive thing to do, but it was the only thing I could think of at the time. Of course now I'm very proud of the Rockefeller name.

Exploring independently, however, I think is very important for the next generation. Even if the intention is to join the family business and participate in the family's philanthropy eventually, getting experience and finding their own way is crucial to becoming more self-assured. We encourage young people to get out and learn – this means they can base solutions on on-the-ground realities, rather than making up solutions from afar.

How does the GPC promote philanthropy among the younger generation?

We have a Next Generation Group for younger members, those in their 20s and 30s, to have their own platform. They discuss issues, such as forming their own identity, that particularly affect them. We also invite social investors and philanthropists whose work is having the most impact to speak to this group about their experiences and hopefully to inspire them.

On the other hand, some of the younger generation are already doing very innovative work, including using social media and other digital tools, or being involved with social enterprises. Our job is to find those at the vanguard who are willing to reach out and take the risk of talking to – and eventually collaborating with – someone from a different sector or someone with a different perspective. By establishing and nurturing these bonds of trust, you have the basis on which to find sustainable solutions to the most pressing problems. ○

A social mission

Caroline Roan

Few elements of a dignified life are as universal as access to good healthcare. Caroline Roan explains how Pfizer, one of the world's largest biopharmaceutical companies, works to answer that call through a corporate responsibility strategy rooted in unconventional partnerships and entrepreneurial problem-solving

———

Caroline Roan
President, Pfizer Foundation

THE AUTHOR

Caroline Roan is president
of the Pfizer Foundation and
vice president of Corporate
Responsibility at Pfizer Inc.
For more than 150 years, the
company has worked to discover
and develop medicines that
significantly improve people's
lives, and deliver those medicines
to patients

B iopharmaceutical companies, especially those that are research-based, have a social mission that goes well beyond the invention, development and commercialisation of advanced medicines and vaccines. Companies like ours are motivated to meet societal expectations to help build the world's capacity to deliver good healthcare and, in particular, to help those who cannot easily access our medicines and vaccines.

We do this in a society that is constantly and rapidly evolving. As the world changes, we and other biopharmaceutical companies are challenged to find fresh approaches to deep-rooted public health issues. The question becomes: how do we look beyond therapeutic advances and philanthropic donations and leverage the entrepreneurial spirit of our colleagues, partners, and even patients, to find more effective ways to meet those challenges?

That means innovating on a scale that no single company can achieve alone, and fostering entrepreneurship in developing and delivering public health solutions at every step. Our solution charts a path of entrepreneurship for good, collaborating with non-traditional partners that share our commitment to designing holistic and lasting public health solutions.

Partnerships are not new on the global stage, but they are an important force in helping companies such as ours address societal needs for access to better healthcare. Through a series of collaborations, we have learned that different global health challenges require different approaches and partnership styles, from long-term commitments designed to combat entrenched diseases to dynamic, market-driven approaches that help to build and strengthen healthcare systems at a national level. We have also discovered a tremendous amount of passion and ingenuity at every level of partnership, and by fostering this potential, we are engaging real people – sometimes even patients themselves – in helping to improve the effectiveness and delivery of healthcare worldwide.

Take, for example, the International Trachoma Initiative (ITI), formed by Pfizer in 1998 in collaboration with the Edna McConnell Clark Foundation, and now a programme of the Task Force for Global Health, an independent non-governmental organisation. The ITI extends to a large group of participants and governments. Our goal is to eliminate blinding trachoma, one of the world's leading causes of preventable blindness, as a serious health threat by 2020, which would represent a landmark achievement in public health. To help reach this goal, we have donated more than 500 million doses of the antibiotic used to treat this devastating disease.

The work of ITI spans more than 17 countries and involves 100 partners and countless individuals who are working every day, in extremely remote areas of the world, to implement a comprehensive public health strategy that looks beyond medicine to eliminate a disease that is exacerbated by poverty. We are a diverse group of non-governmental organisations specialising in blindness, eye care, water and sanitation; academic experts; ministries of health; multilateral organisations; and Pfizer, united around a powerful commitment that crosses cultures, geographic boundaries and sectors. The promise of this partnership is the potential of global elimination of the disease.

ITI is an enormous partnership with impacts to match. Since 1998, the initiative has helped treat approximately 100 million people suffering from trachoma – in fact, our collective efforts resulted in Oman becoming the first country to achieve World Health Organisation (WHO) validation of trachoma elimination and we are on track to meet elimination goals in China, the Gambia, Ghana, Iran, Morocco, Myanmar and Vietnam.

Yet ITI is only one example of the many ways we can join forces with others to foster entrepreneurship for good. Not only do we seek out multi-stakeholder partnerships with organisations, but we also seek out creative problem-solvers who are developing solutions that can have tremendous impact on the healthcare needs of the most vulnerable, and that can be implemented easily in areas where there are fewer resources to work with. We focus on supporting entrepreneurship in many of the countries in which we work. This has the dual benefit of catalysing the private sector and supporting local ingenuity, which together create quality healthcare designed to meet the needs of underserved patients in hard-to-reach areas.

In 2013, the Pfizer Foundation also inaugurated a Health Delivery and Social Innovation portfolio to help catalyse and scale potential high-impact innovations focused on improving health – and especially on connecting underserved patients in low-resource

'As the world changes, we and other pharma companies are challenged to find fresh approaches to deep-rooted public heath issues'

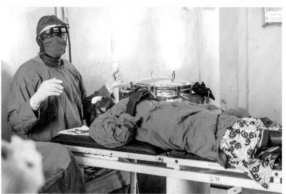

'Our goal is to end blinding
trachoma, one of the world's
leading causes of preventable
blindness, as a serious
health threat by 2020'

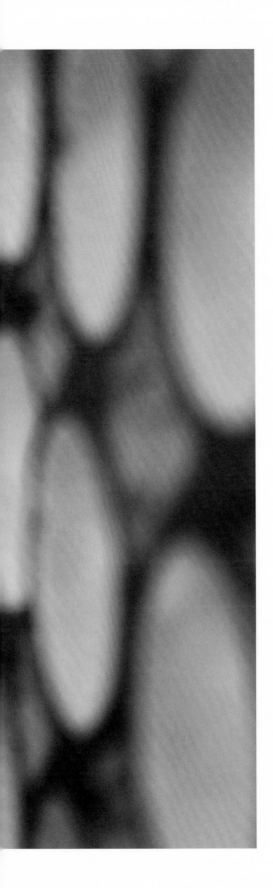

settings, with higher-quality care at an accessible cost. In women's health, for example, we have invested in a jumpstart organisation whose innovations include a low-cost, portable breast cancer-screening device for use virtually anywhere.

We are also supporting a social venture that developed a low-cost, clean birthing kit to prevent infection and reduce maternal and infant mortality. The kit contains simple products manufactured locally by women in India and recommended by the WHO for a clean birth. Another example is our partnership with an organisation that has created a network of roadside clinics at major trucking and transportation crossings to serve hard-to-reach, mobile populations in East Africa. The clinics, created from refurbished shipping containers, provide primary care and sexual and reproductive health counselling, testing and treatment. The organisation uses technology that helps to track patients after they visit, ensuring they get the quality healthcare and follow-up they need. All of these diverse initiatives are driven by passionate individuals and entrepreneurs who are committed to making a difference.

That's something we have in common, and it's what makes these partnerships both possible and powerful. Ultimately, our work alongside both traditional and non-traditional allies, and our commitment to finding and fostering public health entrepreneurs, helps us achieve our business and social mission: ensuring all individuals everywhere have access to quality healthcare and the opportunity to lead healthy lives. ○

"Partnerships are not new, but they are an important force in helping companies such as ours address societal needs"

Changing lives

Sheikha Jawaher Al Qasimi

Conflict and displacement trigger a chain reaction that often leads child victims from poverty, to crime and violence. Sheikha Jawaher bint Mohammed Al Qasimi explains how humanitarian aid must evolve as the needs of refugees do, to break that chain and invest in their education, health and future freedom

————

Sheikha Jawaher Al Qasimi
Eminent advocate for refugee children, UNHCR

————

THE AUTHOR

Sheikha Jawaher bint Mohammed
Al Qasimi is eminent advocate for
refugee children for the United
Nations High Commissioner for
Refugees. She is also the wife of
the Ruler of Sharjah, UAE. In 2013,
she founded the Big Heart UAE
Foundation, which raises funds
for Syrians affected by conflict

———

A courageous young girl named Helen once told me we should look at every war as if it is our family members fighting each other. As a global family, we must find a diplomatic solution to human-made crises. And it is our duty to provide succour to those whose lives have been shattered by conflict. It is for children like Helen that we must shine a light on the global tragedy of displaced men and women – and the children who make up half the world's refugee population.

In the early days my first instinct was to try to help everyone at the same time. But there was always another suffering child or woman I couldn't reach. I learned that it's better to focus our contributions on one objective at a time so that we make a meaningful difference to people's lives. We might not reach every single person who needs help, but if we can lift up some segments of the population, we transform them into humanitarians who in turn will support the people we can't reach.

Over the decades, I have been privileged enough to lead humanitarian efforts from Jordan to Lebanon and Egypt, from Palestine to Somalia and beyond. The brave aid workers I meet have one thing in common: they are ordinary people with extraordinary hearts. However, to make a lasting difference, we – and they – cannot rely solely on emergency aid. You don't teach independence by encouraging dependence. We must invest in their future, through education, as we would invest in the future of any of our children.

Take Syria, the largest humanitarian crisis of our era, and a catastrophe that has occurred so close to my home, the UAE. My biggest concern was that it felt as if the people of Syria had been forgotten and their suffering rendered invisible. Sadly, there is always human tragedy somewhere in the world, so the global media moves on to other breaking news elsewhere. But the refugees will still be homeless after you change the TV channel, and they will still be hungry and traumatised after you turn the newspaper page.

Conflict sets in motion a dangerous chain reaction. Displacement triggers unemployment, which leads to poverty, which in turn forces young refugees into child labour. This leaves them vulnerable to exploitation, crime and violence. Most worryingly, the psychological trauma of seeing their parents killed before their eyes can make children grow up to join the war themselves.

Humanitarian action can break this chain. Yet aid must evolve as the needs of refugees do. When war erupted in Syria, the immediate priority was food, water, blankets and shelter. When days turned into weeks and months became years, it became clear that we should now focus on schools, teachers, books, healthcare and infrastructure and vital counselling to break the cycle of trauma, hate and revenge. Of course the immediate aftermath of a humanitarian crisis will always call for a focus on urgent interventions such as lifesaving medical treatment, but we must not wait too long before embracing more long-term goals.

We can learn lessons from former conflict zones such as Rwanda, where the focus shifted from short-term requirements such as peacekeeping, to medium-term (reuniting displaced families) and then long-term needs (jobs and reconciliation between former enemies). Without this strategic approach, any 'peace' is just a temporary ceasefire and one liable to crumble into conflict again.

For my own part, I saw this in Palestine with my nonprofit initiative Salam Ya Seghar. By helping women to find jobs and supporting female entrepreneurs, we empowered their families indirectly because now the mothers could afford to educate their children. These educated children will grow up and reject crime and violence because they have financial independence. This in turn contributes to peace and gender empowerment.

In Syria, education is not just the gateway to jobs, it is the gateway to peace and tolerance. Good quality schools, teachers and educational material can do more for world peace than all of the world's armies combined. The Big Heart UAE Foundation, which is committed to raising funds for Syrians, and others have already planted the seeds through education, and are determined to ensure that positive success stories emerge from this catastrophe. We need to raise a generation of independent, well educated adults who will rise above their underprivileged background, because what matters is not where they came from, but where they are going. Human history is full of refugees who refused to let their past weigh them down and rose to greatness as Nobel laureates, scientists, writers, educators, artists, inventors and other thought leaders.

Yet this is only possible when we progress from donations to investments in their education, health and freedom. If refugees remain shackled to handouts and aid, we will never know which of those girls and boys might have gone on to great things; to discovering a cure for cancer, tackling world hunger, or negotiating world peace.

I no longer see our work as just charity, because charity implies a one-off aid package to address immediate needs. I see it as an investment in our society and our future. When we educate refugee children, we are creating a generation of adults who will value peace and tolerance. By helping today's refugees, we reduce the ranks of those of tomorrow. o

'Refugees will still be homeless after you change the TV channel, and they will still be hungry and traumatised after you turn the newspaper page'

"When we educate refugee children, we are creating a generation of adults who will value peace and tolerance"

Sheikha Jawaher Al Qasimi

Good returns

Muna Al Gurg

Emirati businesswoman Muna Al Gurg explains how we might harness the immense potential of education and social entrepreneurship, right from the world's refugee camps through to its elite institutions, to engage and empower the next generation of Arab youth

———

Muna Al Gurg
Chairwoman, Young Arab Leaders UAE

————

THE AUTHOR

Muna Al Gurg is a businesswoman and philanthropist. Since 2008 she has been chairwoman of Young Arab Leaders UAE, promoting education and entrepreneurship. She sits on the board of the Al Gurg Foundation and is a founding board member of nonprofit initiatives Hub Dubai and Endeavor UAE

———

Wanting to make a difference is something borne out of a fundamental belief in the power of a good greater than ourselves; in the good that can evolve organically out of concern for the wellbeing of our fellow humans.

As an Arab woman, I find it impossible to sit back and watch – or worse, turn away – as parts of the region suffer through one of the most difficult times in their already troubled history. Millions of innocent people have been displaced from their homes, and millions more driven across national borders into an uncertain and unstable future. Their need for assistance is clear.

As individuals we can only do so much. Yet as individuals who group together with aligned intentions, collectively we have the power to create high-impact initiatives that can change lives for the better. The two areas that I have always believed hold the greatest potential to create sustainable long-term impact are education, and social entrepreneurship. Together they serve every level of the opportunity spectrum; from refugees who are unable to complete their studies, through to existing professionals looking to further their career prospects and fulfil their entrepreneurial vision.

At one end of the scale, there are the vast numbers of refugees living in camps that have evolved from temporary dwellings into makeshift cities. The Za'atari camp in Jordan, with its 80,000 residents, is one of many examples; still more can be found in Lebanon and other nations. Nor is this mass forced migration a challenge that will be faced solely by Syria's neighbours; the political, economic and social fabric of Europe is changing too, as the refugee crisis transcends from a local to a global issue.

These refugees were torn from their daily lives, and many were torn from their educations. With this in mind, organisations such as the Unite Lebanon Youth Project (ULYP) identify children from refugee camps with the potential not only to complete the formal education they would otherwise lose, but then to thrive and succeed in such a way that they may influence those around them. In so doing, they might go on to affect wider positive change in the communities in which they build their futures.

The project has productive links to prestigious institutions such as the American University of Beirut, which has long been regarded as a breeding ground for entrepreneurial success stories. And while education is not the only solution – nor is it a quick fix – the work of ULYP, which I support by funding annual scholarships for students, is directed towards long-term impact. The educations it supports are investments in individuals that may one day benefit the collective. After all, it is better to teach a person to fish, than simply to feed them.

Once individuals have been educated and empowered, with both the knowledge and finance to start their own companies, then they can start thinking about the greater good – at which point, the value of entrepreneurship becomes apparent. Entrepreneurship is powered by dreams and aspirations, vision and ideas. While significant, financial support is far from the most important ingredient for a startup to be successful. More valuable is access to talented, proven mentors and appropriate support networks.

This idea led me to Endeavor, a global nonprofit that empowers high-impact entrepreneurs around the world. Our beneficiaries are not run-of-the-mill businesspeople, but those individuals with the potential to become role models and inspire their colleagues and peers, and entire communities, too. Of course, not every entrepreneur will be successful. Yet by giving the brightest talents access to an unmatched global network of mentors and business leaders, in addition to financial support, we can seed young business leaders with the potential to transform the economies of entire nations. Today's entrepreneurs can identify tomorrow's, and inject the capital that is required to change lives on a huge scale.

I have always believed that success brings with it a responsibility to think about the wider world. In July 2015 I returned to my alma mater, London Business School (LBS), to launch a scholarship that will support students studying on the MBA and Executive MBA programmes. In the same way that a Palestinian or Syrian refugee might complete their studies through ULYP, or a young innovator might receive the guidance they need through Endeavor, I hope that LBS students will be enabled to shape and change attitudes and the future for all, and for the better.

In this increasingly capitalist world, on this unequal and unstable Earth, let us not be applauded into thinking that personal gain is the only goal. Making a difference is about more than that, and the best time to start is now. ○

'Today's entrepreneurs can identify tomorrow's, and inject the capital that is required to change lives on a huge scale'

Building bridges

Alexandre Mars

Making the transition from successful entrepreneur, to successful social entrepreneur is not easy. Alexandre Mars describes his own personal journey after he decided to apply his talents in business to the nonprofit world – fixing a market failure that enables donors and social leaders to deliver positive change

———

Alexandre Mars
Founder, Epic Foundation

————

THE AUTHOR

Alexandre Mars is a serial
entrepreneur and philanthropist
who started his first venture at 17,
and has since launched and sold
several companies. In 2014 he
founded the Epic Foundation to
bridge the gap between donors -
philanthropists, corporations and
foundations - and organisations
supporting children and youth

————

Looking back, the only constant in my career as an entrepreneur has been evolution. Entrepreneurship demands perpetual personal and professional transformation; we are forced into a state of constant adaptation and improvisation in order to survive. This evolution demands of us the humility to pivot, the ability to lead a team in the face of uncertainty, and the foolish curiosity to wander out into a storm when no one else will.

I started my first venture when I was seventeen, running concerts in Paris. With the funds from the concerts I started buying computers and launched web agency A2X. It was the beginning of the internet and we were the crazy people trying to convince everyone that they needed to build a website. Aged twenty, with a ponytail and a beard, I was absolutely convinced we would be successful, but then, nobody called.

Vince Lombardi, the legendary American football coach, is noted for saying to his team: "If you really want to win a game, you need to be on the field." What I realised with A2X was that being an entrepreneur was about being on the field. No-one was going to call me to build a website they didn't know they needed, and we weren't going to keep the lights on without any clients. So, I got on the field. One phone call at a time we started the hard way, building the company into a success and eventually selling it to another agency. Since then I have always stayed on the field; as an entrepreneur it is my home.

In those early days, "It's complicated" would have been the best Facebook status to describe my own relationship with trying to make a difference in the world. Throughout high school and then university, I had always felt torn between what I perceived as two separate spheres. I was becoming ever more involved in giving back to the community while at the same time I was discovering I had a true skill in business. I had contemplated whether the right path was to go immediately to work in politics or nonprofit, or instead to test my emerging passion and aptitude for business. In the end, I chose the second path, thinking I would spend five years as entrepreneur to make money and meet the people I needed to amplify whatever difference I could make.

In reality, though, it didn't take five years but 20 years. Fast forward two decades and I was a proud husband and father to three beautiful children. Now in the process of selling my fourth and fifth startups, I began to think of what would come next. It became clear that now not only as an entrepreneur, but also as a father and a global citizen, I had to evolve again. Having spent the last 20 years in technology, I decided for the first time to venture into a new field, moving from Silicon Valley to the world of social impact. My sixth startup would be a not-for-profit. The challenge was how to set off into a new field at the age of 35. What difference could I really make? Back then I knew almost nothing about philanthropy, nonprofits, social enterprises, monitoring or any of the other wonderful things I would learn about the social sector in the years to come.

Yet, as an entrepreneur, I knew intuitively that the first step was just to get on the field. So I started knocking on doors and

'What was clear to me was that the challenges we as parents were all so worried about would be faced and fought by our children'

doing market research. One after the other I went to foundations and nonprofits saying: "Hi, I want to do some good but I need to understand what it will be." Not every meeting was a success, but I found amazing people who took me under their wings and, in turn, introduced me to more and more people. This journey of discussions and research took place over a three-year period during which I was also exiting my two startups. As the closing of the sales edged closer, the pressure was building quickly to find a way to transition from life as a technology entrepreneur, to life as a social entrepreneur.

Upon selling the companies, my wife Flo and I decided to pull our three kids from their day school for a semester, so we could travel the world together as a family. The trip across 15 countries distilled for me how important it was to support the next generation. Travelling with my own children, we met and lived with families around the world. What was clear to me was that the challenges we as parents were all so worried about would be faced and fought in full by our children. To solve these big global challenges we had to invest in the next generation of global leadership: our children and youth around the world.

As we travelled I also continued my personal research on philanthropy and social impact. Everywhere we went I would speak both with philanthropists looking to make an impact, and teams working each day to make a difference on the ground. As the trip drew to a close it had become increasingly clear just how disconnected these two groups had become.

Paradoxically, in the interconnected Facebook-era world of immediate and constant engagement, what I heard from donors and social leaders across the world was how difficult they found it to connect with each other. On the one hand, we had these incredible organisations and social entrepreneurs spending their days working to solve our most pressing social challenges, but struggling to access the funding, expertise and networks they needed.

Take for example, the CEO of an African agricultural NGO who spends 90 per cent of his time traveling between New York and San Francisco to find donors when his entire operations are on another continent. On the other hand, you have philanthropists and corporations with lots of financial resources and big powerful networks that want to do more but struggle to know who to trust, how to track giving and to how to engage with the organisations they support. This type of market failure was exactly what I had been searching for as an entrepreneur, a clear gap presenting the need for a new organisation to fix it. The good news was that we had a lot of inspiring people who were truly committed to making a difference; now all we had to do was connect them.

The mission of the Epic Foundation is to bridge the gap between those looking to give more, and high-impact NGOs and social enterprises working to empower children and youth globally. We

> ## "As an entrepreneur I knew intuitively that the first step to entering the social sector was just to get on the field"

———

look to create opportunities for everyone to give and do more in support of the next generation, helping our children and youth to be ready to change our world for the better.

Our team achieves this by developing and providing unique new services and technology applications that enable those looking to give more to feel confident they can select trustworthy organisations to support, and that they can truly monitor and experience the results the organisations they support are achieving. I am covering the entire operating cost of Epic Foundation, enabling 100 per cent of donations from other people and companies to go directly to organisations selected to join our portfolio.

Each year we scour the world for the best organisations working to empower children and youth to connect them to our global network of philanthropists and corporations looking to give in a more strategic way. To identify the most impactful organisations, our team has built a new network across the world, of leading foundations, funders and think-tanks. This enabled us to identify and receive applications from more than a thousand organisations across 85 countries in 2015. From the *favelas* of Brazil, to the *banlieues* [suburbs] of Paris, to the bustle of New York City and San Francisco, to the heart of Uganda, to the slums of Mumbai, and the outskirts of Laos, we have searched to find the 20 most trustworthy, innovative, and impactful nonprofits and social enterprises.

At the same time, through merging my passion for entrepreneurship and technology with the best minds in the social sector, we are pushing the envelope in terms of how donors monitor and experience the impact of the organisations they support. We have an amazing team from Manhattan to London to Bangkok that works hand-in-hand with organisations to ensure progress towards agreed social objectives, while providing our donors with more real-time insights on the organisations they support. This new approach is helping unlock critically needed resources, and building a new generation of smarter, more engaged philanthropists.

Over the course of this journey I have learned that we all have different amounts of the same three things to give: our skills, our resources, and our networks. The key to finding the unique impact you can make on the world is to figure out how you can leverage your existing skills, network and resources to make a difference. It is never too early or too late to find the unique opportunity you have to help change the world. ○

'We all have different amounts
of the same three things to
give: our skills, our
resources, and our networks'

Global giving

Jane Wales

Traditionally seen as the preserve of industry leaders from the West, the globalisation of philanthropy has broadened the base of resources – and minds – committed to tackling endemic problems. Jane Wales explains what this means for giving and why the next wave of social innovation will come from the global south

———

Jane Wales
Founder, Global Philanthropy Forum

———

THE AUTHOR

Jane Wales is founder of the
Global Philanthropy Forum,
a peer-learning network of
philanthropists and social
investors with members from 98
countries. She is also CEO of the
World Affairs Council and vice
president of the Aspen Institute,
and has served as acting CEO
of The Elders

———

When the Global Philanthropy Forum (GPF) was first launched in 2001, the word 'global' referred to the focus of our members' giving. We gathered donors and humanitarians mostly from North America to explore opportunities for collaboration on issues of concern overseas. Yet, in the intervening 15 years we have witnessed a seismic shift in our membership that speaks to international trends: the 'global' in our name has come to signify the philanthropists themselves. Philanthropists from Latin America, Asia, Africa and Europe, as well as North America, take part in our annual conference and other activities.

As we move further into the 21st century, the globalisation of philanthropy has important implications for the future of giving. Two significant trends emerge: the rise of innovation in philanthropy from the global south, and an increasing willingness to disregard traditional boundaries – of sectors and disciplines – in the effort to find effective solutions to social ills. These new communities of donors have a palpable sense of a very positive future ahead, and I believe they are the key to making it happen.

The rise of new donors in fast-growing economies is a significant step forward for philanthropy. The next wave of social innovation will come from the global south, in much the same way that microfinance originated in Bangladesh in the 1970s and rapidly spread throughout the rest of the world.

These innovations will be born from a combination of opportunity and need. New wealth is being created by relatively young innovators in emerging markets. Many are energised to 'do good' with that wealth. At the same time there are pressing social needs on their doorstep, for inequality remains an unhappy feature of the global economy. The inequities affect us all.

At the GPF, we have concentrated most recently on building the African Philanthropy Forum (APF), a community of Africa's strategic philanthropists and social investors. The APF provides an opportunity for African philanthropists to engage, inform and guide global donors' giving in Africa, to influence positively the philanthropic dollars coming to the continent. But more than that, this community is coalescing around the idea that Africa can be the source of some of the most inventive philanthropy from which the rest of the world can learn. They can imagine a not-too-distant future in which Africa meets its own development needs, in part because of socially conscious high-net-worth-individuals.

Moreover, these leaders are already partnering with counterparts and across sectors. Take, for example, Nigeria's Aliko Dangote, founder of the Dangote Group and eponymous foundation. The Dangote Foundation – in collaboration with the Bill & Melinda Gates Foundation, Rotary International and agencies such as the UN children's agency – contributed significantly to the campaign to eradicate polio in Nigeria. His philanthropy helped pay for the training of healthcare workers, the building of clinics and the gathering of data. When Ebola struck in West Africa, Nigeria was able to address the outbreak before it became an epidemic, partly because the country could repurpose the infrastructure and capability that had been established.

Public-private partnerships such as these have a long history, most notably going back to the Green Revolution of the 1970s. Yet what is striking is the ease with which new philanthropists adopt this approach. They are not concerned with boundaries of any sort, whether geographic, sector or disciplinary. This impetus is evident in organisations such as the Global Fund to fight AIDS, TB and Malaria, the vaccine alliance Gavi, and others.

There are challenges ahead, to be sure. Philanthropists and foundations have the freedom to focus on systems change and long-term benefits, unconstrained by political or market pressures. They have access to data that can help them hone their strategies and intervene with greater precision and to greater effect. But evidence on what works is gathered and weighed over the long term, and many of the dangers philanthropy seeks to address are immediate. In those instances, we rely on philanthropy to take risks. This is a field that will always struggle to maintain a delicate balance between proven strategies and audacious bets to make a real difference now.

Private donors now comprise an increasingly global philanthropic community with a sense of purpose. In gatherings of philanthropists, I am struck by their combination of pragmatism and felt moral obligation. Their generosity and willingness to take on hard problems is matched only by the determination and inventiveness of those they support. The combination portends a brighter future. ○

"Philanthropy will always struggle to maintain a delicate balance between proven strategies and audacious bets to make a real difference"

Beyond rhetoric

Kate Roberts

Women and girls hold the key to ending extreme poverty and
inequality. Yet, they are held back as much by cultural norms as lack
of access to services. Kate Roberts, cofounder of Maverick Collective,
describes how ideas and innovations are just as important as funding
in the fight for change

———————

Kate Roberts
Cofounder, Maverick Collective

———————

THE AUTHOR

Kate Roberts is the cofounder of Maverick Collective and a senior vice president at Population Services International, where she led successful public health initiatives to increase public awareness around HIV. She is also an adjunct professor on social entrepreneurship at George Washington University

——

O n most mornings I'm woken by my energetic five-year-old daughter, Lilly, bounding into my bed. As I look into her eyes, I always reflect on the thousands of girls I've met on my journey, and the hardships that many have endured. While my daughter will certainly face challenges in her life, many girls in the developing world face a much steeper climb, and one that begins on the very day they are born.

Those challenges can include surviving birth, receiving proper nutrition, getting an education, avoiding child marriage and early pregnancy, and much more. A girl is often held back by cultural norms that don't value her contribution to society. Essential services such as care during and post-pregnancy are harder to come by, especially for women in rural areas. Every day in 2015, the World Health Organisation estimated that 830 women died due to complications of pregnancy and childbirth. No mother should die giving life.

Twenty years before Lilly was born, I was working in the private sector, advertising and marketing cigarettes and bubblegum, and travelling the globe. I had spent 10 years in that world before I made a business trip to South Africa in 1999. There I caught sight of another world, one in stark contrast to my own comfortable life. The poverty was overwhelming and the beginning of the HIV and AIDS crisis meant that there were increasing numbers of funerals in these poor communities. I had an epiphany: that not only did I have to try to right some of these inequalities, but that the private sector with which I was so familiar could be a powerful tool in achieving that goal.

Shortly after my return from South Africa I joined Population Services International (PSI), a US-based global health nonprofit with more than 9,000 staff and operations in 70 countries. PSI is focussed on the power and potential of girls and women, and I wanted to harness this to develop a new approach to ending poverty in our lifetime. In 2012, Princess Mette-Marit of Norway and I visited India as part of our work advocating for girls and women. We were each disappointed by the amount of talk and lack of action we saw: organisations would put the needs of girls and women on the agenda of the international development community, yet funding so rarely matched rhetoric.

Maverick Collective was our response. It is an initiative born of both frustration and hope: frustration that precious resources and talent were being left on the table as organisations were not engaging with women philanthropists; but also hope that we can learn from each other and build a new model of philanthropy to truly amplify impact and create new champions for girls and women. We were inspired by Melinda Gates, a great example of a woman using her voice and resources to put family planning on the global agenda, and so we were honoured when she joined our nascent effort as co-chair.

Our initiative brings together a diverse and global group of philanthropists, who are passionate, committed and innovative. The 14 founding members are invested in this new approach to philanthropy, where members are engaged in the programmes they support, bringing not only their financial commitment but their expertise and voice as well. We are piloting new approaches, learning from them, leveraging our learning with others, and scaling successful approaches to reach as many girls and women as we possibly can.

To achieve this we are committed to transparency at every level of every programme. This maximises our members' ability to identify new solutions to difficult challenges: they are able to intervene directly in the many projects in which we are involved. Take Pam Scott, a hugely successful marketing executive who has inspired companies such as Nike and Levi's to better understand their consumers through human-centred design. She brought the same approach to our programmes in Tanzania, so that we might better understand teen pregnancy from the girls' perspective, and develop solutions that give these young women access to the contraceptive services they need and want.

We tell all our members that it is ok to 'fail fast' so that we can learn quickly and change our approach to ensure the maximum impact. In Pam's case in Tanzania, we piloted several ideas in quick succession. Some failed, but the learnings ultimately helped us succeed. Pam's design approach has since inspired the creation of a $30m initiative across three countries, led by PSI and funded by the Bill & Melinda Gates Foundation and the Children's Investment Fund Foundation.

Another Maverick Collective member, Indrani Goradia, was raised in a strict household in Trinidad and Tobago. She was a victim of abuse for many years, and it took her a long time to realise that she could make a difference to the many other women affected by gender-based violence. Like all of us, Indrani was deeply affected by the brutal rape and torture of Jyoti Singh on a Delhi bus in 2012. Rolling up her sleeves, Indrani invested herself in a gender-based violence programme to test novel approaches to preventing violence and supporting survivors in India, a country where 40 million women are abused every day.

Indrani's approach brings together local organisations, engages boys and men, and connects community leaders with policymakers for a coordinated response. The programme is changing attitudes and it has changed Indrani, too: she is now a fearless leader and a fierce, public advocate for women's safety. Two years after we launched the programme, our key learnings inspired the US government to partner with us and make ours the largest gender-based violence programme in India. We have been able to expand our activities, reach more girls and women, and amplify our impact in preventing and addressing violence across the country.

Maverick Collective is an initiative of PSI and therefore benefits from PSI's reach, depth of knowledge, technical expertise, and

'Maverick Collective was born of the hope we can learn from each other and build a new philanthropy to amplify impact'

global resources. This means members don't have to establish infrastructure, develop local partnerships and recruit the technical expertise needed to achieve high impact. Instead they are able to engage deeply from day one, using their voice to advocate and inspire, and their intellect to innovate and find new approaches to tackling serious issues. So far we have reached 300,000 girls and women and leveraged $60m for programmes across the developing world. New members are joining, including men, which sends a powerful message that men too want what's right for girls and women.

When Lilly was born I made a promise to her that I would do everything in my power to change the future for girls and women around the world. The bottom line is that investing in girls and women is the fastest way to end extreme poverty, yet money alone does not solve generations-old problems or address endemic inequalities. We need ideas and we need innovations, and at Maverick Collective we are putting our resources, expertise and voices behind this very objective. ○ .

'We were disappointed by the amount of talk and lack of action for girls and women. Funding so rarely matched rhetoric'

Photos:
Alwaleed Philanthropies; Bill & Melinda Gates
Foundation; Carter Center; David Goff; Education for
Employment; Epic Foundation; Freedom Fund; Getty Images;
Jacob Balzani Lööv; Jessica Hilltout; Jo Pugliese;
Kanouté Foundation; Legatum Foundation; Mark Seliger;
MasterCard Foundation; Matt Walker; MSF; Pfizer
Foundation; Roll Back Malaria; Shutterstock; Synergos;
UNHCR; UN Women; Verko Ignjatovic; Water.org; WPDI